DevOps Revolution

Transforming Software Delivery for High-Performance Teams

Ryan Campbell

Table of Contents

How to Use This Book

Navigating Your DevOps Journey

This book is designed to guide you through a comprehensive exploration of the DevOps revolution. Whether you're a seasoned professional or new to the concept, the following steps will help you make the most of this resource:

1. **Start with the Basics:** If you're new to DevOps, begin with the introduction and foundational chapters to establish a clear understanding of the core principles.

2. **Tailor Your Learning:** Feel free to dive into chapters that align with your current knowledge level and objectives. Each chapter is designed to be informative and actionable on its own.

3. **Engage with Practical Examples:** Case studies, real-world scenarios, and examples throughout the book will help you grasp the practical application of DevOps principles.

4. **Apply What You Learn:** Use the insights gained from each chapter to enhance your software delivery practices. Experiment with tools, methodologies, and cultural shifts discussed.

5. **Continuous Learning:** DevOps is an evolving field. Stay engaged with the latest trends and innovations by exploring the final chapter on future trends and innovations.

6. **Reflect and Discuss:** Take advantage of the discussion points and reflective exercises provided in each chapter to internalize the concepts and share insights with your team.

Embark on your DevOps journey with confidence, and transform your software delivery process into a high-performance engine of innovation and efficiency.

Introduction

Embracing the DevOps Revolution

In an era where software powers our daily lives and drives businesses forward, the quest for efficient, reliable, and agile software delivery has become paramount. The DevOps revolution stands at the forefront of this transformation, offering a new paradigm that redefines how software is developed, delivered, and maintained.

Understanding the Evolution of Software Delivery

The journey from conception to deployment of software has undergone a remarkable evolution. From the days of manual code compilation to the era of rapid, continuous deployment, the landscape has shifted dramatically. In this book, we embark on a historical voyage, tracing the trajectory of software delivery methodologies. Wc'll explore the challenges that arose with traditional siloed approaches, leading to the birth of DevOps as a response to the ever-increasing demands for speed, collaboration, and quality.

The Core Principles of DevOps

At its heart, DevOps embodies a set of core principles that transcend organizational boundaries and empower teams to break down barriers. Collaboration, communication, automation, and continuous improvement form the cornerstones of this philosophy. We'll delve into each principle, dissecting its significance and uncovering the ways in which they synergistically drive software delivery efficiency. By embracing these principles, organizations can foster a culture of shared responsibility, mutual respect, and relentless pursuit of excellence.

Benefits of Adopting DevOps Practices

The adoption of DevOps practices brings forth a cascade of transformative benefits. From accelerated development cycles to reduced error rates, the impact of DevOps resonates throughout the software development lifecycle. As we progress through this book, we'll shed light on the tangible advantages that await those who embrace DevOps. Whether you're a developer, a system administrator, a quality assurance professional, or a business leader, the rewards of implementing DevOps practices extend to every facet of your role.

Join us as we embark on a captivating exploration of DevOps—a movement that has reshaped the software industry's landscape. Through insightful analysis, real-world case studies, and actionable guidance, "DevOps Revolution" equips you with the knowledge and tools to drive high-performance teams and revolutionize your approach to software delivery.

Prepare to revolutionize your software delivery practices and embrace the DevOps journey like never before. The future of software development starts here.

Chapter 1: Foundations of DevOps

Defining DevOps: A Holistic Approach

In the fast-paced world of software development, where code evolves into applications and systems that power our digital lives, a new approach has emerged – DevOps. But what exactly is DevOps, and why has it taken the tech industry by storm? In this section, we'll unravel the layers of DevOps, breaking down its core concepts in a way that's easy to understand, even if you're new to the world of software development.

The Birth of DevOps

Imagine a world where developers and operations teams exist in separate silos, each focusing solely on their domain. Developers write code, while operations handle deployment and maintenance. It might seem logical, but this separation often leads to inefficiencies, miscommunications, and bottlenecks.

DevOps was born out of the need to bridge this gap, to foster collaboration and enhance the software delivery process. It's not just a set of practices; it's a cultural shift that brings developers and operations professionals together, working as a cohesive unit to achieve common goals.

The Holistic Philosophy

At its core, DevOps is a holistic philosophy that promotes a shift from isolated, linear processes to a unified, circular approach. It's like a finely tuned orchestra where each instrument plays a unique role, but the beauty emerges when they synchronize their efforts.

In the world of software, this means that developers, operations, quality assurance, security, and other stakeholders join forces from the very beginning. This approach ensures that everyone's insights and expertise contribute to the entire software lifecycle, from concept to delivery and beyond.

Collaboration at Every Stage

DevOps isn't just about writing code and deploying it. It's about collaboration at every stage of the software development lifecycle. Imagine a scenario where developers and operations teams work closely from the start, discussing requirements, infrastructure, and deployment strategies. This collaboration helps to identify potential challenges early on, reducing the risk of surprises later in the process.

For instance, when a developer writes a piece of code, they have the operations perspective in mind – how will this code run in a production environment? Simultaneously, operations professionals provide valuable input on scalability, security, and infrastructure, guiding the development process.

Continuous Integration and Continuous Deployment (CI/CD)

A crucial element of the DevOps approach is the concept of Continuous Integration and Continuous Deployment, often abbreviated as CI/CD. This practice involves automating the building, testing, and deployment of code changes. In simpler terms, every time a developer makes a code change, it's automatically integrated into a shared repository, tested thoroughly, and if all tests pass, deployed to production.

CI/CD eliminates the old, manual process of writing code, handing it over to another team, and hoping for the best. Instead, it ensures that changes are small, frequent, and thoroughly vetted. This not only reduces the chances of introducing bugs but also accelerates the pace of development.

Embracing Automation

DevOps embraces automation to achieve efficiency and consistency. Think of automation as your trusty assistant, taking care of repetitive and time-consuming tasks, leaving you free to focus on more creative and strategic aspects of software development.

Automation covers various aspects, from setting up development environments to deploying applications and monitoring performance. By automating these processes, DevOps teams can ensure that every deployment is consistent, reducing the likelihood of "it works on my machine" scenarios.

The Three-Way Model

To truly understand DevOps, let's explore the Three-Way Model – a fundamental concept that represents the three main principles of DevOps: Flow, Feedback, and Continual Learning & Experimentation.

1. **Flow:** This refers to the movement of code changes from development to production. DevOps emphasizes optimizing this flow to ensure that changes are delivered quickly and smoothly, without bottlenecks.

2. **Feedback:** Feedback is the heartbeat of DevOps. It involves continuously collecting data and insights from various stages of the software delivery process. This feedback loop informs teams about the impact of their changes, enabling them to make informed decisions for improvement.

3. **Continual Learning & Experimentation:** DevOps encourages a culture of learning and experimentation. This means embracing failure as an opportunity to learn, being open to new ideas, and constantly seeking ways to refine and enhance processes.

In Summary

DevOps is not just a buzzword; it's a fundamental shift in how we approach software development. It's about tearing down walls between teams, fostering collaboration, embracing automation, and continuously striving for excellence. By adopting a holistic approach to software delivery, DevOps empowers organizations to innovate faster, respond to challenges more effectively, and ultimately deliver better software products to their users.

Remember, DevOps isn't a one-size-fits-all solution. It's a mindset, a philosophy that adapts to your organization's unique needs and goals. As we journey through this book, you'll gain a deeper understanding of the DevOps principles and practices that can transform the way you approach software development. So, fasten your seatbelt, and let's embark on this transformative DevOps journey together.

Cultural Shifts and Collaboration

Building Bridges in the DevOps World

In the realm of DevOps, technological advancements are only part of the equation. A significant aspect of its success lies in the cultural shifts it promotes and the emphasis it places on collaboration. In this section, we'll explore how DevOps challenges traditional silos and cultivates a culture that fosters communication, cooperation, and shared responsibility.

Breaking Down the Silos

Picture a traditional software development environment: developers on one side, operations on the other. Communication between these two groups is often limited, leading to misunderstandings, delays, and inefficiencies. DevOps seeks to shatter these silos, creating a more interconnected and dynamic ecosystem.

When developers and operations professionals collaborate from the outset, the entire software delivery process becomes a cohesive journey. The walls that once separated departments crumble, replaced by bridges of understanding and shared goals. This cultural transformation not only improves efficiency but also injects a sense of camaraderie and joint ownership into the development process.

Communication as a Cornerstone

It's not just about exchanging messages; it's about fostering clear and open lines of communication between teams that historically operated in isolation.

Imagine developers and operations engineers huddled together, brainstorming solutions and sharing insights. Instead of relying on occasional meetings, real-time communication tools become the norm. Discussions about requirements, code changes, infrastructure needs, and deployment strategies flow seamlessly, ensuring everyone is on the same page.

Shared Responsibility, Shared Success

DevOps goes beyond collaboration; it encourages shared responsibility. When developers and operations professionals work as a cohesive unit, successes and challenges are shared collectively. This mindset shift leads to a more holistic understanding of the software delivery process.

For example, if a production issue arises, the blame game fades into oblivion. Instead, the team rallies together to diagnose the issue, find a solution, and ensure it doesn't recur. This shift from finger-pointing to joint problem-solving nurtures a culture of trust, where mistakes are viewed as opportunities for improvement.

Automating Routine Tasks

Another cultural shift brought by DevOps is the adoption of automation to handle routine, repetitive tasks. This doesn't replace human expertise; rather, it liberates teams from the drudgery of manual labor, freeing them to focus on higher-value activities.

By automating tasks such as code integration, testing, and deployment, teams can accelerate the development cycle. This leads to quicker releases, fewer errors, and enhanced collaboration. Automation becomes a unifying force, enabling both developers and operations professionals to contribute their expertise towards the creation of a seamless and efficient pipeline.

The Power of Empathy

Perhaps one of the most profound cultural shifts instilled by DevOps is the cultivation of empathy. Developers gain insight into the challenges faced by operations teams, and vice versa. This understanding breeds patience, respect, and a willingness to support one another.

Developers learn to consider the operational implications of their code, leading to more efficient deployments. Operations professionals gain appreciation for the intricacies of software development, aiding in better decision-making regarding infrastructure and performance.

Embracing the DevOps Culture

In the ever-evolving landscape of software delivery, a strong foundation of collaboration and cultural alignment is paramount. DevOps doesn't just introduce technological changes; it revolutionizes how teams work together. By breaking down silos, promoting communication, encouraging shared responsibility, automating routine tasks, and nurturing empathy, DevOps empowers organizations to achieve operational excellence and drive innovation.

As we navigate the DevOps landscape, keep in mind that this cultural shift is an integral part of the journey. By embracing a DevOps culture, you're not just adopting a methodology; you're becoming part of a movement that empowers teams to reach new heights of collaboration, efficiency, and success.

Automation and Continuous Integration: Paving the Fast Lane to DevOps Success

In the world of DevOps, where speed, quality, and efficiency reign supreme, automation and continuous integration emerge as the dynamic duo that propels software delivery to new heights. In this section, we'll delve into the significance of automation and how continuous integration forms the backbone of a streamlined DevOps process.

The Automation Advantage

Imagine a world where manual, repetitive tasks are automated, freeing up human resources for more creative and strategic endeavors. This is the promise of automation in DevOps. It's not about replacing human expertise; it's about amplifying it by offloading routine chores to machines.

Automation comes into play at various stages of the software development lifecycle. Code compilation, testing, deployment, and infrastructure provisioning – these are just a few areas where automation can make a monumental difference. By scripting and orchestrating these tasks, DevOps teams ensure consistency, accuracy, and repeatability.

Continuous Integration: The Heartbeat of DevOps

At the core of DevOps lies the practice of continuous integration (CI). Picture a seamless conveyor belt where code changes are integrated and tested continuously. CI hinges on the principle of small, frequent code integrations as opposed to infrequent large-scale ones.

With CI, as developers make code changes, those changes are automatically integrated into a shared repository. This swift integration helps uncover bugs and conflicts early in the development process, preventing the dreaded "integration hell" scenario that often arises when multiple developers work on different branches for extended periods.

The CI Process Unveiled

Let's walk through the CI process step by step:

1. **Code Changes:** Developers write code and make changes to existing codebases.

2. **Automated Build:** Once changes are pushed to the repository, an automated build process kicks in. This process compiles the code, checks for errors, and prepares it for testing.

3. **Automated Testing:** Various automated tests are conducted to ensure the code functions as expected. These tests cover unit tests, integration tests, and even user interface tests.

4. **Immediate Feedback:** If any issues are detected during testing, feedback is provided immediately, allowing developers to address problems promptly.

5. **Deployment to Staging:** Once the code passes all tests, it's deployed to a staging environment where further testing and validation occur.

6. **Validation and Verification:** The code is rigorously tested in the staging environment to ensure it behaves as expected and doesn't adversely impact the existing system.

7. **Deployment to Production:** After passing all tests and validations, the code is deployed to the production environment. This process occurs swiftly and confidently due to the confidence gained from rigorous testing at earlier stages.

The Virtuous Cycle of CI/CD

Continuous Integration doesn't stop at testing; it merges seamlessly into Continuous Deployment (CD). CD extends the automation pipeline beyond testing to the actual deployment of code changes to production environments.

This virtuous cycle creates a rhythm of small, frequent changes that undergo rigorous testing before being confidently deployed. The result? An agile development process that minimizes risks, accelerates innovation, and ensures high-quality software delivery.

The Future of Automation and CI

As technology evolves, the landscape of automation and continuous integration continues to expand. From the rise of containerization and microservices to the integration of AI and machine learning into testing processes, the future holds exciting possibilities.

Embracing automation and continuous integration isn't just about staying ahead in the DevOps race; it's about revolutionizing the way software is developed, tested, and delivered. By automating routine tasks and adopting a culture of continuous integration, DevOps teams create a foundation of efficiency and reliability that empowers them to excel in the ever-evolving world of software development.

Chapter 2: Agile Development and DevOps

Synergy Between Agile and DevOps: A Perfect Partnership for Software Excellence

In the dynamic realm of software development, two powerhouse methodologies have emerged to drive innovation, speed, and quality: Agile and DevOps. Individually, each approach revolutionized the industry; together, they form an unbeatable alliance that propels software delivery to new frontiers. In this section, we'll explore the profound synergy between Agile and DevOps, uncovering how their harmonious collaboration sets the stage for software excellence.

Agile: The Seeds of Speed and Flexibility

At its core, Agile is all about adaptability and responsiveness. It's a mindset that challenges the traditional, rigid approach to software development. Agile methodologies, such as Scrum and Kanban, advocate iterative and incremental development. Instead of crafting exhaustive plans upfront, Agile teams embrace change and welcome customer feedback throughout the development process.

Agile principles introduce concepts like user stories, sprints, and regular retrospectives. The emphasis is on delivering value to users in small, frequent increments. This approach ensures that software remains aligned with user needs and market dynamics, driving higher customer satisfaction and reducing time-to-market.

DevOps: The Orchestra of Collaboration and Continuity

Enter DevOps, a methodology that amplifies Agile's principles by harmonizing development and operations. DevOps doesn't just focus on the speed of code delivery; it encompasses the entire software lifecycle, from conception to deployment and beyond.

The synergy between Agile and DevOps is rooted in collaboration. Agile teams develop features at a rapid pace, and DevOps ensures these features are seamlessly integrated, tested, and deployed. Gone are the days of disjointed handoffs between development and operations; instead, Agile and DevOps teams collaborate in real time, sharing insights and expertise.

Embracing the Agile-DevOps Bridge

The Agile-DevOps partnership is fueled by shared values and aligned goals:

1. **Customer-Centricity:** Both Agile and DevOps revolve around meeting customer needs and delivering value. Agile captures user requirements through iterative feedback loops, while DevOps ensures rapid delivery of these requirements without compromising quality.

2. **Iterative Development:** Agile's iterative approach seamlessly merges with DevOps' continuous integration and deployment practices. This combination enables teams to release features swiftly while maintaining a robust feedback mechanism.

3. **Transparency and Communication:** Agile's emphasis on communication aligns seamlessly with DevOps' culture of collaboration. Cross-functional teams communicate openly, breaking down silos and fostering a culture of shared responsibility.

4. **Quality Assurance:** Agile focuses on delivering high-quality increments, and DevOps complements this by providing automated testing and deployment pipelines. This ensures that quality isn't sacrificed in the pursuit of speed.

Achieving Unprecedented Efficiency

The Agile-DevOps synergy manifests in various ways:

- **Rapid Feedback Loops:** Agile teams gather feedback from users, which informs development. DevOps ensures this feedback is rapidly integrated into the software, allowing for swift adjustments.

- **Continuous Improvement:** Agile's retrospectives and DevOps' focus on continual learning create a loop of refinement. Teams continuously enhance their processes, resulting in increased efficiency over time.

- **Faster Time-to-Market:** By integrating Agile's iterative development with DevOps' continuous deployment, organizations can release features faster, capturing market opportunities swiftly.

The Future: A Harmonious Symphony

As software development evolves, the relationship between Agile and DevOps will only deepen. The future holds promises of even tighter integration, seamless tooling, and an enhanced focus on end-to-end automation.

In essence, Agile and DevOps join forces to create a dynamic, responsive, and efficient software delivery machine. Together, they empower organizations to embrace change, drive innovation, and deliver software that not only meets user expectations but also exceeds them. The synergy between Agile and DevOps is more than a partnership; it's a powerful alliance that paves the way for software excellence in an ever-evolving digital landscape.

Agile Methodologies and DevOps Practices: A Symbiotic Evolution for Rapid Innovation

In the quest for rapid, customer-focused software delivery, two transformative forces have emerged: Agile methodologies and DevOps practices. These methodologies, though distinct, share a symbiotic relationship that amplifies their impact on the software development landscape. In this section, we'll explore how Agile methodologies and DevOps practices intertwine, creating a harmonious blend that drives innovation, efficiency, and excellence.

Agile Methodologies: A Foundation of Flexibility

Agile methodologies, epitomized by approaches like Scrum, Kanban, and Extreme Programming (XP), revolutionized software development by championing adaptability, collaboration, and customer-centricity.

Scrum: Scrum divides development into time-bound iterations called sprints. Cross-functional teams work on small, prioritized units of work (user stories) within each sprint. This iterative approach fosters collaboration, regular feedback, and the delivery of functional, incremental software.

Kanban: Kanban focuses on visualizing and optimizing workflow. Tasks are represented on a Kanban board, allowing teams to manage work in progress and respond swiftly to changing priorities.

XP (Extreme Programming): XP emphasizes technical excellence through practices like test-driven development (TDD), pair programming, and continuous integration. It promotes a disciplined approach to coding and encourages close collaboration between developers.

DevOps Practices: The Orchestra of Continuous Delivery

DevOps practices, on the other hand, concentrate on the seamless integration of development and operations. DevOps acts as the enabler that transforms Agile's iterative development into a continuous delivery powerhouse.

Continuous Integration (CI): CI is the heartbeat of DevOps. Automated tests validate these integrations, ensuring that changes are of high quality and reducing the likelihood of integration conflicts.

Continuous Delivery (CD): Building upon CI, CD takes automation a step further. Once code passes tests, it's automatically deployed to production or staging environments. This end-to-end automation ensures that software changes are swiftly and reliably delivered to users.

A Harmonious Blend

The synergy between Agile methodologies and DevOps practices is evident in their shared goals and complementary principles:

1. **Frequent Deliveries:** Agile's iterative approach aligns seamlessly with DevOps' emphasis on frequent code integration and deployment. This collaboration enables teams to deliver small, valuable features consistently.

2. **Collaboration:** Agile's cross-functional teams merge naturally with DevOps' culture of collaboration between developers and operations professionals. Communication flows freely, reducing misunderstandings and delays.

3. **Feedback Loops:** Agile methodologies employ feedback loops through retrospectives and customer interactions. DevOps extends this by incorporating feedback into the development pipeline, enabling rapid adjustments.

4. **Quality Assurance:** Agile's focus on delivering high-quality increments aligns with DevOps' automated testing and deployment. This ensures that code changes are thoroughly vetted and reliable.

The Result: Accelerated Innovation

The marriage of Agile and DevOps creates a virtuous cycle of rapid innovation:

1. **Agile's Speed:** Agile methodologies drive quick, incremental changes based on user feedback.

2. **DevOps' Efficiency:** DevOps practices enable swift and automated integration, testing, and deployment of these changes.

3. **Immediate Feedback:** The combination leads to rapid feedback, allowing teams to adapt and enhance their work swiftly.

4. **Innovation Amplified:** This cycle of rapid feedback and iteration fuels a culture of continuous improvement and innovation.

A Path Forward

As software development evolves, the interplay between Agile methodologies and DevOps practices will continue to evolve. This partnership, rooted in flexibility, collaboration, and efficiency, will shape the future of software delivery. By embracing the symbiotic evolution of Agile and DevOps, organizations can harness the power of rapid innovation and deliver software that delights users and propels businesses forward.

Accelerating Iterations with DevOps: A Fast Lane to Iterative Excellence

In the fast-paced world of software development, where change is the only constant, the ability to iterate swiftly and efficiently is paramount. Enter DevOps, a methodology that turbocharges the iterative process, enabling teams to iterate faster, smoother, and with greater confidence. In this section, we'll explore how DevOps serves as a catalyst for accelerating iterations, amplifying innovation, and driving continuous improvement.

Streamlining Development Lifecycles

DevOps shatters the traditional barriers between development, testing, and deployment. Instead of moving sequentially from one phase to another, DevOps encourages a parallel and interconnected approach.

Automated Testing: DevOps emphasizes automated testing throughout the development process. As code is written, automated tests are executed, catching issues early and enabling swift corrective actions.

Continuous Integration: Developers frequently integrate their code into a shared repository. This frequent integration, backed by automated testing, ensures that changes are small, manageable, and consistently validated.

Reducing Bottlenecks and Delays

In traditional development setups, bottlenecks often arise during the integration and testing phases. These bottlenecks delay progress and result in costly rework.

Early Detection of Issues: With continuous integration and automated testing, issues are identified and addressed promptly. This eliminates the need for large-scale troubleshooting efforts and accelerates the development pace.

Efficient Conflict Resolution: DevOps' focus on small, frequent integrations minimizes the chances of code conflicts. If conflicts do arise, they're easier to manage due to the smaller scope of changes.

Continuous Deployment: The Ultimate Accelerant

DevOps doesn't stop at continuous integration; it extends into continuous deployment (CD). CD automates the deployment process, ensuring that validated code changes reach production environments swiftly and reliably.

Automated Deployment Pipelines: CD streamlines the path to production with automated deployment pipelines. Once code passes automated tests, it's automatically deployed, eliminating manual intervention and potential errors.

Faster Feedback Loops: The swift deployment enabled by CD means that user feedback is gathered sooner. This feedback informs the next iteration, leading to rapid adjustments and improvements.

Amplifying Agile's Iterative Approach

DevOps and Agile methodologies are like two gears perfectly meshed to drive iterative excellence.

Agile's Incremental Development: Agile emphasizes delivering small increments of value to users. DevOps ensures that these increments are swiftly integrated, tested, and deployed, making the Agile approach even more potent.

Rapid and Continuous Innovation: The combined force of DevOps and Agile empowers teams to innovate at an unprecedented pace. Changes are quickly conceptualized, developed, tested, and released, enabling organizations to seize opportunities and stay ahead in dynamic markets.

A Culture of Continuous Improvement

Perhaps the most remarkable aspect of accelerating iterations with DevOps is its transformative effect on organizational culture.

Rapid Feedback Loops: DevOps' emphasis on swift iterations fosters a culture of immediate feedback. Teams learn from each iteration, identifying what works, what doesn't, and how to improve.

Experimentation and Innovation: Accelerated iterations provide more opportunities for experimentation. DevOps teams can test new features, gather data, and iterate based on real-world insights, fostering a culture of innovation.

The Journey Ahead

As software development evolves, the synergy between DevOps and rapid iterations will continue to evolve. Emerging technologies, automation advancements, and continuous learning will further propel the iterative process.

By embracing DevOps' ability to accelerate iterations, organizations position themselves at the forefront of innovation. They tap into a rhythm of swift development, rigorous testing, and rapid deployment that ensures software evolves at the pace of change – a pace that is nothing short of transformative in the ever-evolving landscape of technology.

Chapter 3: Building a High-Performance DevOps Team

The DevOps Mindset and Team Dynamics: Catalyzing Collaboration and Continuous Improvement

In the dynamic landscape of software delivery, success isn't solely determined by tools and processes. The DevOps mindset and team dynamics play a pivotal role in fostering a culture of collaboration, adaptability, and relentless pursuit of excellence. In this section, we'll delve into the intricacies of the DevOps mindset and how it shapes team dynamics, accompanied by prime examples that highlight its transformative impact.

The DevOps Mindset: From Silos to Synergy

The DevOps mindset is a departure from traditional siloed thinking. It's a paradigm shift that encourages teams to transcend departmental boundaries and work together as a cohesive unit.

Example: Collaborative Cross-Functional Teams

Imagine a software development team composed of developers, testers, and operations professionals. In a traditional setup, these roles often work in isolation, leading to miscommunications and delays. In a DevOps-aligned team, these roles collaborate from the outset. Developers write code with operations considerations in mind, testers provide feedback on functionality, and operations professionals contribute insights on deployment and scalability. This cohesive approach ensures that each team member's expertise is leveraged throughout the software development lifecycle, resulting in faster, more reliable outcomes.

Team Dynamics: The Power of Shared Ownership

DevOps thrives on a culture of shared ownership, where every team member takes responsibility for the end-to-end delivery process.

Example: Incident Response and Blameless Post-Mortems

In a traditional setting, when a production incident occurs, blame often becomes the focal point. DevOps teams, however, adopt a blameless approach. When an incident occurs, the focus shifts from assigning blame to understanding what went wrong and how to prevent it in the future. Team members collaborate to conduct post-mortems, analyzing the incident's root causes and suggesting improvements. This approach not only fosters a culture of continuous learning but also reinforces the idea that everyone shares the responsibility for maintaining a reliable and resilient system.

Continuous Improvement: Learning from Failure

The DevOps mindset embraces failure as an opportunity for growth and learning. Instead of fearing mistakes, teams view them as stepping stones towards improvement.

Example: Netflix Chaos Monkey

Netflix, a pioneer in DevOps practices, developed a tool called Chaos Monkey. This tool intentionally injects failures into their production environment. Why? To test the system's resiliency and the team's response to unexpected incidents. When Chaos Monkey triggers a failure, the team collaborates to resolve the issue swiftly and learns valuable lessons in the process. This culture of learning from failure has enabled Netflix to build a robust, highly available system that can withstand real-world challenges.

Continuous Feedback: Nurturing a Culture of Openness

The DevOps mindset values feedback loops at every stage of the software delivery process, fostering a culture of transparency and open communication.

Example: Continuous Integration and Automated Testing

Consider a scenario where a developer introduces a bug into the codebase. In a DevOps environment, continuous integration pipelines automatically detect the issue and provide immediate feedback to the developer. This fast feedback loop enables the developer to address the problem before it progresses further in the development cycle. The result is higher code quality and fewer defects reaching production.

The Transformational Impact

Embracing the DevOps mindset and cultivating effective team dynamics isn't just a theoretical endeavor; it's a transformative journey that yields tangible benefits:

- Enhanced Collaboration: Teams collaborate seamlessly, leveraging each other's strengths for holistic software delivery.

- Rapid Adaptability: DevOps teams respond swiftly to changing requirements, market dynamics, and user feedback.

- Continuous Learning: A culture of continuous improvement encourages teams to refine processes based on real-world insights.

- Resilience and Innovation: By learning from failures and embracing experimentation, teams build more resilient systems and drive innovation.

In the ever-evolving landscape of software delivery, the DevOps mindset and effective team dynamics stand as the pillars of success. When combined with cutting-edge tools and processes, they create a harmonious symphony that propels organizations towards unprecedented levels of collaboration, efficiency, and excellence.

Cross-Functional Collaboration and Skill Sets: Nurturing a Unified DevOps Ecosystem

In the ever-evolving realm of software development, where complexity reigns and user expectations soar, the ability to forge a unified team of diverse skill sets is more critical than ever. DevOps, a philosophy that transcends traditional departmental boundaries, places cross-functional collaboration at the heart of its success. In this section, we'll delve into the nuances of cross-functional collaboration within DevOps, exploring its transformative impact on skill sets, team dynamics, and ultimately, the software delivery process.

The Essence of Cross-Functional Collaboration

Cross-functional collaboration in the context of DevOps is akin to assembling a well-rounded orchestra. Each instrument brings a unique sound, and only when harmoniously combined does the music come to life. Similarly, in DevOps, various skill sets come together to orchestrate a seamless software delivery process.

Example: The DevOps Symphony

Imagine a DevOps team comprising developers, testers, operations engineers, security experts, and data analysts. Traditionally, these roles might have operated in silos. However, in a DevOps environment, they collaborate to ensure every aspect of software development is addressed comprehensively. Developers write code, testers ensure functionality and quality, operations professionals handle deployment and infrastructure, security experts safeguard against vulnerabilities, and data analysts gather insights for continuous improvement. This unified effort results in a refined, high-quality end product.

Skill Sets: The Diverse Ensemble

DevOps thrives on a diverse set of skills, each contributing a vital piece to the puzzle.

Development: Developers write the code that forms the foundation of software applications. Their expertise lies in crafting clean, efficient code that fulfills user requirements.

Testing and QA: Testers ensure the software functions as intended by conducting various tests – from unit tests that validate individual components to user acceptance tests that assess the overall functionality.

Operations and Infrastructure: Operations professionals manage the infrastructure and deployment pipelines. Their skill sets include configuring servers, optimizing performance, and automating deployment processes.

Security: Security experts safeguard the software against vulnerabilities and cyber threats. They ensure that sensitive data is protected and implement best practices to prevent breaches.

Data Analytics: Data analysts gather insights from user behavior and system performance. These insights drive informed decisions for enhancements and optimizations.

Breaking Down Silos: The Collaborative Advantage

Traditionally, these skill sets might have functioned independently, leading to bottlenecks and misunderstandings. DevOps smashes these silos, fostering seamless collaboration.

Example: Integrating Security Early

In a traditional model, security might be an afterthought, leading to vulnerabilities that are discovered late in the process. In a DevOps environment, security experts collaborate with developers from the outset. This early integration ensures that security measures are embedded in the code from the start, reducing risks and enabling faster, secure deployments.

Skill Set Enrichment: The Power of Exposure

In DevOps, team members are exposed to a broader spectrum of skills. Developers gain insights into deployment and operations, operations engineers learn about coding practices, and testers understand security implications.

Example: Cross-Training for Empowerment

Imagine a DevOps engineer who specializes in operations but also learns coding skills. This cross-training equips them to contribute to coding tasks when needed. Similarly, a developer might explore infrastructure management, enhancing their understanding of how code functions in a live environment.

The Transformative Impact

The fusion of diverse skill sets through cross-functional collaboration yields transformative benefits:

- **Enhanced Problem Solving:** Teams approach challenges from multiple angles, leveraging their combined expertise to find innovative solutions.

- **Reduced Bottlenecks:** Cross-functional teams can swiftly address bottlenecks, as different skill sets collaborate to resolve issues.

- **Higher-Quality Outcomes:** Collaborative efforts lead to more comprehensive testing, robust security measures, and efficient deployment practices.

- **Continuous Learning:** Exposure to diverse skills nurtures a culture of continuous learning, where team members expand their horizons and enhance their capabilities.

Skill Set Evolution: The Learning Continuum

DevOps thrives on a learning continuum. As technology evolves, skill sets must adapt.

Example: Cloud Native Expertise

With the rise of cloud computing, operations professionals need expertise in managing cloud infrastructure. This skill set evolution is essential for effective DevOps practices, ensuring that teams stay aligned with technological trends.

Bridging Skill Set Gaps: The Power of Mentorship

In cross-functional teams, knowledge transfer becomes a natural process. Senior team members mentor junior members, helping bridge skill set gaps.

Example: Gradual Exposure

A junior developer working in a DevOps team gains exposure to automation tools, deployment processes, and infrastructure management. Guided by senior colleagues, they gradually build proficiency in these areas.

The Future of Skill Sets in DevOps

As the software landscape evolves, skill sets will continue to evolve. Emerging technologies like AI and machine learning will introduce new areas of expertise.

Example: AI-Driven Operations

AI will likely play a significant role in operations. Operations engineers will need expertise in configuring AI-powered systems that monitor, analyze, and optimize software performance.

Conclusion: A Harmonious Ensemble

In the symphony of DevOps, cross-functional collaboration and diverse skill sets create a harmonious ensemble that drives innovation and excellence. By fostering a culture where team members share knowledge, break down silos, and embrace continuous learning, organizations ensure that their software delivery process remains in tune with the ever-evolving demands of technology.

Nurturing a Culture of Learning and Improvement: The Cornerstone of DevOps Evolution

In the relentless march of technology, where change is constant and innovation is imperative, organizations that embrace a culture of continuous learning and improvement stand poised for success. DevOps, a philosophy rooted in agility and adaptability, places immense value on this culture as a driving force for excellence. In this section, we'll delve into the profound significance of nurturing a culture of learning and improvement within the DevOps framework, exploring how it fosters innovation, empowers teams, and propels organizations to the forefront of software delivery.

The Essence of Continuous Learning

Continuous learning is more than a buzzword; it's a mindset that fuels growth and innovation. In the context of DevOps, continuous learning is woven into the fabric of every action, decision, and interaction.

Example: Retrospectives for Reflection

Imagine a DevOps team that conducts regular retrospectives after each iteration. During these sessions, team members reflect on what went well, what could be improved, and potential solutions. This process not only encourages open communication but also instills a sense of ownership and responsibility for continuous improvement.

Fostering an Environment of Curiosity

A culture of learning encourages team members to ask questions, experiment, and explore new territories.

Example: Hackathons and Innovation Days

Some organizations dedicate time for hackathons or innovation days, during which team members are free to explore new technologies, experiment with ideas, and share their findings. This environment of curiosity breeds innovation, allowing teams to uncover novel solutions and technologies that enhance their DevOps practices.

Encouraging Experimentation

A culture of learning empowers teams to experiment and iterate fearlessly.

Example: Blue-Green Deployments

Imagine an operations team exploring the concept of blue-green deployments, a technique where two identical production environments (blue and green) are maintained. New releases are deployed to the green environment, which is then switched to production once validated. The team experiments with this approach, learning its benefits and challenges. If successful, the knowledge gained is shared, and blue-green deployments become a standard practice, enhancing deployment reliability.

Continuous Improvement: A Mindset, Not a Destination

DevOps embraces the idea that improvement is a journey, not a destination. Teams are encouraged to seek opportunities for enhancement at every turn.

Example: Pipeline Optimization

Consider a DevOps team that manages deployment pipelines. While the pipeline is functional, the team recognizes that it could be more efficient. Instead of settling for the status quo, they engage in a process of continuous improvement. By introducing parallel processing for testing stages and optimizing resource allocation, they significantly reduce deployment time and enhance overall efficiency.

Building a Feedback-Driven Culture

A culture of learning thrives on feedback. Teams actively seek input, both internally and externally, to drive improvement.

Example: User Feedback Integration

Incorporating user feedback is central to DevOps principles. When a new feature is released, the team monitors user reactions and gathers insights. Based on this feedback, they iterate on the feature, enhancing its usability and value.

Learning from Failure: Turning Setbacks into Successes

In a culture of learning, failure is not feared but embraced as a stepping stone to success.

Example: Learning from Post-Mortems

When a production incident occurs, a DevOps team conducts a post-mortem to understand its root causes and prevent recurrence. This approach transforms a setback into an opportunity for learning and improvement. The insights gained from these post-mortems are integrated into the development and deployment process, enhancing the system's reliability.

Empowering Teams through Learning

A culture of continuous learning empowers teams by providing opportunities for skill enhancement and personal growth.

Example: Professional Development Allowances

Some organizations allocate budgets for professional development, allowing team members to attend conferences, workshops, or online courses. These opportunities not only enhance individual skills but also enrich the team's collective knowledge.

The Transformational Impact

Nurturing a culture of learning and improvement within DevOps yields transformative results:

- **Innovation:** Teams become incubators of innovation, constantly exploring new tools, techniques, and practices.

- **Resilience:** By learning from failures and adapting, teams build resilient systems that can withstand challenges.

- **Agility:** A culture of learning prepares teams to swiftly adapt to technological shifts and market demands.

- **High Morale:** Teams engaged in continuous learning feel valued, motivated, and inspired.

The Journey Ahead: Lifelong Learning

In the ever-evolving landscape of technology, the pursuit of knowledge is a lifelong journey.

Example: Staying Abreast of Cloud Technologies

As cloud technologies evolve, DevOps teams must continuously learn about new services, best practices, and security measures. This ongoing learning ensures that teams maximize the benefits of cloud computing while safeguarding against potential pitfalls.

Conclusion: Thriving in Change

In the digital era, where disruption is the norm, the ability to learn, adapt, and improve is a distinguishing factor. DevOps, with its emphasis on agility and collaboration, serves as a fertile ground for cultivating a culture of continuous learning and improvement. By embracing this culture, organizations not only remain relevant but also thrive amidst change, ensuring that their software delivery process remains innovative, efficient, and aligned with the ever-evolving needs of the industry.

Chapter 4: The Seamlessness of Integration and Uninterrupted Delivery

Streamlining Code Integration and Testing: Unleashing the DevOps Engine of Quality

In the fast-paced realm of software development, the ability to seamlessly integrate code changes and rigorously test them is paramount. DevOps, a methodology renowned for its emphasis on automation and collaboration, places great importance on streamlining these processes. In this section, we will delve deep into the intricacies of code integration and testing within the DevOps framework, exploring how automation, continuous testing, and efficient collaboration synergize to propel software quality to new heights.

The Challenge of Code Integration

In traditional software development, code integration is often a cumbersome process, prone to conflicts, delays, and quality issues.

Example: Merge Nightmares

Imagine a project where multiple developers are working on different features simultaneously. As the project nears its release date, the code from these different branches needs to be integrated into a single, cohesive codebase. However, integrating diverse code changes can lead to conflicts, where different pieces of code interact unpredictably. Resolving these conflicts becomes a laborious process that stalls progress and introduces errors.

The DevOps Solution: Continuous Integration

DevOps introduces a game-changing solution: continuous integration (CI). CI involves frequently integrating code changes into a shared repository, followed by automated testing to ensure the changes don't introduce defects.

Example: Automated CI Pipelines

In a DevOps environment, developers commit their code changes multiple times a day. These changes trigger automated CI pipelines that include comprehensive tests – from unit tests that validate individual components to integration tests that ensure proper interaction between modules. If the code passes all tests, it's considered suitable for further integration and deployment.

Benefits of Continuous Integration

CI's impact on code integration is revolutionary:

- **Early Issue Detection:** Automated tests catch issues early, when they're easier and less expensive to fix.

- **Reduced Integration Conflicts:** Frequent integration reduces the size and complexity of code changes, minimizing conflicts.

- **Rapid Feedback:** Developers receive rapid feedback on their code changes, fostering a culture of quality and accountability.

- **Enhanced Collaboration:** CI encourages collaboration by promoting a shared repository, where code changes are visible to the entire team.

The Challenge of Rigorous Testing

Thorough testing is essential for delivering high-quality software. However, traditional testing methods can be slow and error-prone.

Example: Manual Testing Bottlenecks

Consider a scenario where a QA team manually tests each new feature. As the codebase grows, the number of features to be tested increases, potentially leading to testing bottlenecks. Manual testing is time-consuming, and human errors can result in missed defects.

The DevOps Solution: Continuous Testing

DevOps amplifies testing through continuous testing (CT). CT involves automating testing processes to ensure comprehensive coverage and rapid feedback.

Example: Automated Regression Testing

In a DevOps setup, automated regression tests are created to validate existing functionality with each new code change. As code is integrated, these tests are executed, ensuring that new features don't inadvertently break existing functionality.

Benefits of Continuous Testing

CT's impact on software quality is profound:

- **Comprehensive Test Coverage:** Automated tests cover a wide range of scenarios, ensuring robust functionality.

- **Faster Feedback:** Rapid test execution provides immediate feedback, enabling swift issue resolution.

- **Regression Prevention:** Automated regression tests catch regressions before they reach production.

- **Efficient Resource Utilization:** Automation reduces the need for manual testing, allowing QA teams to focus on more complex scenarios.

Collaborative Synergy: Developers and Testers Unite

DevOps thrives on collaboration between developers and testers.

Example: Shift Left Testing

In DevOps, testing isn't relegated to the end of the development cycle. Instead, testing is "shifted left," meaning it starts earlier in the process. Developers write automated tests as they code, ensuring that their changes are validated immediately. This collaborative approach minimizes defects and accelerates the development process.

DevOps Testing Ecosystem

DevOps integrates an array of testing practices:

- **Unit Testing:** Validating individual components in isolation.

- **Integration Testing:** Verifying interactions between components.

- **End-to-End Testing:** Simulating user scenarios to ensure complete system functionality.

- **Performance Testing:** Assessing system performance under various conditions.

Automation Elevation: The Power of Tools

Automation tools are the backbone of efficient code integration and testing in DevOps.

Example: Jenkins for Continuous Integration

Jenkins, a popular automation server, enables teams to set up CI/CD pipelines. It automates code integration, testing, and deployment, ensuring a seamless and consistent process.

The Transformative Impact

The synergy of streamlined code integration and continuous testing yields transformative results:

- **Higher Quality:** Automated tests catch defects early, resulting in higher-quality software.

- **Faster Delivery:** Rapid integration and testing reduce time-to-market.

- **Reduced Risk:** Rigorous testing minimizes the likelihood of critical defects reaching production.

- **Innovation Encouragement:** Automation frees developers and testers to focus on innovation rather than repetitive tasks.

Challenges and Pitfalls

While DevOps-enhanced code integration and testing offer immense benefits, challenges exist:

- **Automation Complexity:** Implementing automation tools requires expertise and effort.

- **Test Maintenance:** Automated tests must be regularly updated to remain relevant.

- **Cultural Shift:** Teams accustomed to manual processes may resist automation.

Conclusion: The DevOps Quality Engine

Streamlining code integration and testing is more than a process improvement; it's a cultural shift that transforms how software quality is achieved. By embracing continuous integration, continuous testing, and collaboration between developers and testers, DevOps empowers organizations to deliver software that meets the highest standards of quality, efficiency, and innovation. In the race for software excellence, the DevOps quality engine stands as a driving force that propels organizations toward a future where quality is not just an aspiration, but an inherent component of every code change and every deployment.

Automated Deployment Pipelines: Orchestrating DevOps Magic for Swift and Reliable Delivery

In the fast-paced landscape of software delivery, where the demand for rapid and error-free deployments is paramount, automated deployment pipelines emerge as a cornerstone of DevOps success. These pipelines orchestrate the intricate dance of code changes, testing, and deployment, ensuring that software reaches production swiftly and reliably. In this section, we will delve into the intricacies of automated deployment pipelines within the DevOps framework, unveiling how they streamline processes, enhance quality, and empower teams to deliver with confidence.

The Imperative for Swift and Reliable Deployments

Traditional deployment processes often involve manual steps, human intervention, and the potential for errors.

Example: Manual Deployments

Imagine a scenario where a development team has completed a new feature. In a traditional setup, deploying this feature to the production environment involves multiple manual steps: copying files, configuring databases, and adjusting settings. This manual process is not only time-consuming but also prone to inconsistencies and mistakes.

The DevOps Solution: Automated Deployment Pipelines

DevOps responds to the challenge of deployments with automated deployment pipelines. These pipelines automate the end-to-end process of taking code changes from development to production.

Example: Continuous Deployment Pipeline

In a DevOps environment, developers commit code changes to a version control system. These changes trigger an automated pipeline that includes not only testing but also deployment. If the code passes all tests, it's automatically deployed to a staging environment for further validation. Once validated, the same pipeline promotes the code to the production environment. This seamless, automated process reduces the risk of errors and accelerates deployment.

Benefits of Automated Deployment Pipelines

Automated deployment pipelines offer substantial benefits:

- **Consistency:** Automated pipelines ensure that the same steps are followed every time, reducing the risk of configuration errors.

- **Efficiency:** Manual tasks are replaced with automated processes, reducing deployment time and freeing teams from repetitive tasks.

- **Reduced Risk:** Automated deployments minimize human errors that can lead to defects in production.

- **Swift Feedback:** Automated testing and deployment provide rapid feedback on code changes, fostering a culture of continuous improvement.

The Challenge of Configuration Management

Maintaining consistent configurations across different environments is a common challenge.

Example: Configuration Drift

Consider a situation where a configuration setting is manually adjusted in the staging environment to troubleshoot an issue. If this change isn't documented and replicated in the production environment, configuration drift occurs. The production environment becomes inconsistent with staging, potentially leading to defects.

The DevOps Solution: Infrastructure as Code (IaC)

DevOps tackles configuration management with infrastructure as code (IaC). IaC involves defining infrastructure configurations in code, which can be versioned, tested, and deployed just like application code.

Example: IaC Templates

Using tools like Terraform or CloudFormation, DevOps teams define infrastructure components – servers, databases, networks – in code.

This code is then used to provision and configure environments consistently across staging, testing, and production.

Benefits of Infrastructure as Code

IaC offers numerous advantages:

- **Consistency:** IaC ensures that environments are identical, reducing the risk of configuration-related defects.

- **Versioning:** IaC code is versioned, providing transparency into changes and facilitating rollbacks if needed.

- **Efficiency:** IaC automates environment setup, minimizing manual configuration efforts.

- **Scalability:** IaC simplifies scaling by allowing teams to define and replicate infrastructure components easily.

Collaborative Pipelines: Developers and Operations Unite

Automated deployment pipelines foster collaboration between development and operations teams.

Example: DevOps as a Bridge

Traditionally, developers focused on writing code, while operations teams managed deployment and infrastructure. In a DevOps setup, these roles merge. Developers write code with deployment considerations, while operations engineers collaborate on the pipeline's infrastructure elements. This cross-functional collaboration ensures that the deployment pipeline addresses both technical and operational aspects.

Continuous Deployment vs. Continuous Delivery

Two deployment models often discussed in DevOps are continuous deployment and continuous delivery.

Continuous Deployment: In this model, code changes are automatically deployed to production as soon as they pass automated tests. This approach requires a high degree of testing automation and confidence in the code's quality.

Continuous Delivery: Here, code changes are automatically deployed to staging environments. From there, they can be manually promoted to production after validation. Continuous delivery maintains the rapid deployment process while allowing teams to exercise additional caution before releasing to production.

Automated Deployment Pipeline Components

An automated deployment pipeline comprises several components:

- **Source Control:** Code changes are managed and versioned in a source control system like Git.

- **Build and Test:** Automated build processes compile code and run automated tests.

- **Artifact Repository:** Compiled code and dependencies are stored in an artifact repository.

- **Staging Environment:** An environment where code changes are deployed for validation.

- **Production Environment:** The live environment where validated code changes are deployed for end users.

The Transformative Impact

The integration of automated deployment pipelines into DevOps practices yields transformative outcomes:

- **Rapid Delivery:** Automated pipelines expedite code changes from development to production.

- **Quality Assurance:** Automated testing within pipelines ensures that code changes meet quality standards.

- **Efficiency:** Manual deployment tasks are replaced with automated, repeatable processes.

- **Risk Reduction:** Automated processes minimize human errors that can lead to production defects.

Challenges and Best Practices

While automated deployment pipelines offer substantial benefits, they require careful planning and execution:

- **Testing Strategy:** Rigorous automated testing is essential to ensure that code changes don't introduce defects.

- **Security:** Security measures must be integrated into deployment pipelines to safeguard against vulnerabilities.

- **Monitoring and Rollback:** Monitoring tools and rollback procedures should be in place to swiftly address unexpected issues in production.

Conclusion: The DevOps Accelerator

Automated deployment pipelines embody the essence of DevOps – a seamless blend of automation, collaboration, and quality assurance. These pipelines empower organizations to deliver software with unprecedented efficiency and reliability. By embracing the orchestration of code changes, testing, and deployment through automated pipelines, DevOps practitioners propel

Chapter 5: Infrastructure as Code (IaC)

Infrastructure Automation Principles: The Engine Driving DevOps Agility

In the ever-evolving landscape of technology, where the demand for scalable, reliable, and efficient infrastructure is paramount, infrastructure automation emerges as the bedrock of DevOps success. The principles of automating infrastructure provisioning, configuration, and management are at the heart of building agile, adaptable, and resilient systems. In this section, we will delve into the core principles of infrastructure automation within the DevOps framework, unveiling how they empower organizations to harness the full potential of their technological landscape.

The Challenge of Manual Infrastructure Management

Traditional infrastructure management often involves manual, error-prone processes.

Example: Manual Server Provisioning

Consider a scenario where an organization needs to deploy a new application. In a conventional setup, this might require manually configuring servers, installing software, and setting up networking. This approach is time-consuming, subject to human errors, and lacks scalability.

The DevOps Solution: Infrastructure as Code (IaC)

DevOps transforms infrastructure management with the paradigm of Infrastructure as Code (IaC). IaC treats infrastructure components as code, enabling automated provisioning, configuration, and management.

Example: IaC Templates

IaC leverages tools like Terraform or Ansible to define infrastructure components using code. This code, known as templates, is versioned, tested, and deployed in a consistent and automated manner.

Benefits of Infrastructure as Code

IaC offers substantial benefits to infrastructure automation:

- **Consistency:** IaC ensures that environments are reproducible and identical, reducing the risk of configuration discrepancies.

- **Scalability:** IaC enables easy scaling by replicating infrastructure components.

- **Version Control:** IaC code is versioned alongside application code, facilitating transparency, collaboration, and rollbacks.

- **Efficiency:** IaC automates provisioning and configuration tasks, accelerating deployment.

Immutability: Treating Infrastructure as Immutable

Immutability is a principle that advocates treating infrastructure as immutable entities. Instead of modifying existing components, new instances are created and configured.

Example: Immutable Servers

Imagine a situation where a new version of an application is released. In an immutable infrastructure, new servers with the updated application are provisioned, while the old servers are decommissioned. This approach minimizes configuration drift, simplifies rollbacks, and enhances reliability.

Automation-First Mindset: Automate Everything

In DevOps, automation isn't a supplementary endeavor; it's a guiding principle. The automation-first mindset encourages teams to automate every repetitive, error-prone, and time-consuming task.

Example: Continuous Integration and Continuous Deployment

In an automation-first approach, continuous integration and continuous deployment pipelines are fully automated. From code integration to testing to deployment, every step is orchestrated through automated tools and scripts.

Idempotency: Repeatability in Automation

Idempotency is a fundamental principle that ensures automation operations can be executed multiple times with the same result, regardless of the initial state.

Example: Configuration Management

In a DevOps environment, configuration management tools ensure idempotency. For instance, a configuration script that installs a software package checks if it's already installed before proceeding. This ensures that running the script multiple times won't result in unwanted changes.

Testing Infrastructure: Treating Infrastructure as Code

Just as application code undergoes rigorous testing, so should infrastructure code. Infrastructure testing involves validating that IaC templates work as intended.

Example: Infrastructure Testing Frameworks

DevOps teams use tools like Kitchen-Terraform or ServerSpec to test infrastructure code. These tools simulate deployments and configurations, ensuring that infrastructure changes are predictable and reliable.

Orchestration: Coordinating Complex Processes

Orchestration involves coordinating multiple automation tasks to achieve complex outcomes.

Example: Multi-Tier Application Deployment

Deploying a multi-tier application involves provisioning servers, configuring load balancers, setting up databases, and more. Orchestration tools like Kubernetes or Docker Swarm automate this complex process, ensuring consistent and coordinated deployments.

Continuous Monitoring and Remediation

In a dynamic infrastructure landscape, continuous monitoring is essential to ensure stability and performance.

Example: Infrastructure Monitoring Tools

Tools like Prometheus or Nagios continuously monitor servers, networks, and applications. If an issue is detected, automated remediation scripts can be triggered to resolve the problem.

Secure Automation: Integrating Security

Automation shouldn't compromise security. Security measures must be seamlessly integrated into automated processes.

Example: Automated Security Scanning

Automated security scanning tools can assess infrastructure components for vulnerabilities during provisioning. If vulnerabilities are found, the automation pipeline can halt until the issues are resolved.

Collaboration: Bridging Development and Operations

Example: DevOps Collaboration

In a DevOps culture, developers and operations engineers collaborate on IaC templates. Developers define infrastructure requirements in templates, and operations engineers ensure that these templates align with operational best practices.

The Transformative Impact

Embracing infrastructure automation principles yields transformative results:

- **Agility:** Automated provisioning and scaling empower organizations to swiftly adapt to changing demands.

- **Reliability:** Immutability and idempotency minimize configuration errors and enhance system stability.

- **Efficiency:** Automation accelerates provisioning, configuration, and management tasks, reducing manual efforts.

- **Scalability:** Infrastructure as Code enables efficient scaling without manual intervention.

Challenges and Best Practices

While infrastructure automation offers immense benefits, challenges must be addressed:

- **Complexity:** Automation tools require expertise to implement and manage.

- **Version Control:** IaC templates must be versioned alongside application code to ensure synchronization.

- **Testing Rigor:** Infrastructure code must undergo thorough testing to avoid configuration-related defects.

Conclusion: The Automation Engine

Infrastructure automation principles lie at the heart of the DevOps movement, propelling organizations towards unprecedented levels of agility, scalability, and reliability. By embracing Infrastructure as Code, immutability, orchestration, and an automation-first mindset, organizations tap into a wellspring of transformative potential. In an era where infrastructure is as dynamic as the applications they support, these principles stand as the automation engine that drives the DevOps revolution, enabling organizations to navigate the complex landscape of technology with confidence and innovation.

Benefits of Infrastructure as Code (IaC) in DevOps: Empowering Agility and Quality

In the dynamic landscape of software development and IT operations, the adoption of Infrastructure as Code (IaC) emerges as a pivotal enabler of DevOps success. IaC not only revolutionizes how infrastructure is provisioned and managed but also aligns seamlessly with the core tenets of agility, collaboration, and continuous improvement that define DevOps. In this section, we will delve into the multifaceted benefits that IaC brings to the DevOps ecosystem, shedding light on how it accelerates deployment, enhances reliability, fosters collaboration, and empowers organizations to navigate the ever-changing technological terrain.

Rapid and Reproducible Deployment

IaC's most apparent benefit lies in its ability to expedite the deployment process while ensuring reproducibility across environments.

Example: Swift Scaling

In a DevOps environment, as demand surges, organizations need to scale their infrastructure swiftly. IaC templates allow for automated provisioning of new servers, databases, and networking components, ensuring that scalability is achieved without the laborious manual setup.

Example: Consistent Testing Environments

Developers and testers often require identical environments for testing and development. With IaC, these environments can be spun up quickly using the same templates, eliminating discrepancies and ensuring consistent testing.

Enhanced Reliability through Consistency

IaC's emphasis on consistency has a profound impact on system reliability.

Example: Minimized Configuration Drift

Configuration drift – variations between environments due to manual changes – is a common source of defects. IaC mitigates this risk by ensuring that configurations are codified and applied uniformly across environments. Changes are made in the IaC templates, reducing the chances of discrepancies.

Example: Idempotent Changes

IaC templates are designed to be idempotent – running them multiple times produces the same outcome. This ensures that the infrastructure is always in the desired state, regardless of the number of times changes are applied.

Collaboration and Version Control

IaC is a potent catalyst for collaboration between development and operations teams.

Example: Code Collaboration Practices

In a DevOps culture, infrastructure code is treated like application code. It's stored in version control systems like Git, enabling developers and operations engineers to collaborate on changes, review code, and maintain version history.

Example: Pull Requests for Infrastructure

Pull requests, commonly used in software development, are extended to infrastructure code. Operations engineers can review and approve changes before they are merged, ensuring that infrastructure modifications align with operational requirements.

Enhanced Auditing and Compliance

IaC augments auditing and compliance efforts, ensuring that infrastructure adheres to security and regulatory standards.

Example: Transparent Changes

When all infrastructure changes are tracked in version control, organizations gain transparency into who made what changes and when. This traceability aids in auditing and compliance reporting.

Example: Automated Compliance Checks

IaC templates can include automated checks to ensure that infrastructure configurations adhere to security policies and compliance standards. This proactive approach reduces the risk of non-compliant deployments.

Efficient Disaster Recovery and Rollbacks

IaC streamlines disaster recovery and rollbacks, essential components of maintaining system availability and minimizing downtime.

Example: Immutable Infrastructure for Recovery

In a disaster recovery scenario, IaC enables rapid recovery by provisioning new infrastructure instances using the same templates. Since infrastructure is defined in code, restoring the entire system to a functional state becomes achievable in a shorter timeframe.

Example: Rollbacks Made Easier

When issues arise after a deployment, rolling back changes becomes simpler with IaC. Reverting to a previous version of the IaC template ensures that the entire environment is reverted to a known state.

Enabling Infrastructure Testing

Just as software undergoes rigorous testing, IaC enables testing of infrastructure components.

Example: Infrastructure Test Suites

DevOps teams can develop and execute infrastructure test suites to validate IaC templates. These tests ensure that infrastructure changes are predictable, reliable, and aligned with desired outcomes.

Example: Pre-Deployment Validation

Automated tests can be integrated into the deployment pipeline, validating infrastructure changes before they are applied. This proactive validation minimizes the risk of deployment failures due to faulty infrastructure.

Cost Optimization and Resource Efficiency

IaC contributes to cost optimization and efficient resource management.

Example: Cost-Effective Scaling

IaC allows organizations to scale infrastructure based on demand. As traffic increases, additional resources can be provisioned using pre-defined templates. When demand subsides, these resources can be deprovisioned, avoiding unnecessary costs.

Example: Resource Tagging and Management

IaC can include resource tagging, enabling organizations to track resource usage and allocate costs accurately. This level of visibility assists in optimizing resource allocation and budget planning.

Holistic DevOps Transformation

IaC isn't merely a technical change; it's a catalyst for a broader DevOps transformation.

Example: Cultural Shift

Embracing IaC necessitates a cultural shift where development and operations teams collaborate closely. This cultural alignment, in turn, fuels a holistic DevOps mindset that values agility, communication, and continuous improvement.

Implementing Infrastructure as Code (IaC) Tools and Best Practices: Building the Foundation for DevOps Excellence

The adoption of Infrastructure as Code (IaC) is a pivotal step in embracing the DevOps philosophy. While the principles of IaC promise transformative benefits, effectively implementing IaC requires a strategic approach, the right tools, and adherence to best practices. In this section, we will delve into the essential components of implementing IaC, exploring the selection of tools, the establishment of workflows, the cultivation of reusable templates, and the incorporation of security measures. By following these best practices, organizations can build a robust foundation for DevOps excellence and unlock the full potential of IaC.

Choosing the Right IaC Tools

The first step in implementing IaC is selecting the appropriate tools that align with your organization's needs and preferences.

Example: Terraform and Ansible

Terraform and Ansible are two popular IaC tools. Terraform focuses on declarative provisioning of infrastructure, while Ansible emphasizes configuration management through automation.

Example: Cloud-Specific Tools

Cloud providers offer their IaC tools, such as AWS CloudFormation or Google Cloud Deployment Manager. These tools integrate seamlessly with their respective platforms and services.

Infrastructure as Code Workflows

Implementing IaC requires well-defined workflows that encompass development, testing, and deployment.

Example: Git-Flow for IaC

Adopting a Git-based workflow is common for managing IaC code. Developers work on feature branches, create pull requests, and merge changes into a main branch. Continuous integration pipelines are triggered for automated testing and validation.

Example: Environments and Deployment

IaC workflows should delineate the deployment process across environments. Changes should be promoted from development to staging to production, with each deployment involving automated provisioning and configuration.

Infrastructure Templates: The Backbone of IaC

Reusable infrastructure templates are the heart of IaC. These templates define infrastructure components as code.

Example: Terraform HCL

Terraform uses HashiCorp Configuration Language (HCL) to define infrastructure. HCL templates describe resources, their configurations, and relationships.

Example: Ansible Playbooks

Ansible uses YAML-based playbooks to describe configuration tasks. Playbooks define the desired state of systems and the tasks required to achieve that state.

Version Control and Collaboration

IaC templates, like application code, should be stored in version control systems to facilitate collaboration and versioning.

Example: Git Repositories

IaC templates should reside in Git repositories, enabling versioning, change tracking, and collaboration among development and operations teams.

Example: Pull Requests for IaC

Enforcing a pull request workflow for IaC changes allows for code review, validation, and collaboration before changes are merged and deployed.

Continuous Integration and Continuous Deployment (CI/CD)

Incorporating IaC into your CI/CD pipelines ensures that infrastructure changes are tested and validated before reaching production.

Example: Automated Testing

CI/CD pipelines should include automated tests for IaC templates. These tests validate that templates generate the expected infrastructure and configurations.

Example: Infrastructure Validation

IaC changes should be validated in staging environments before deployment to production. Automated tests should verify that infrastructure changes align with operational requirements.

Security and Compliance Integration

Security measures should be integrated into IaC implementations to ensure that infrastructure is deployed securely and compliantly.

Example: Security Scans

Incorporate security scanning tools that assess IaC templates for vulnerabilities, misconfigurations, and compliance violations before deployment.

Example: Automated Compliance Checks

IaC templates can include automated checks for compliance with security policies and industry regulations, reducing the risk of non-compliant deployments.

Secret Management and Configuration

Handling sensitive data and configurations securely is crucial in IaC implementations.

Example: Secret Management Tools

Integrate tools like HashiCorp Vault or AWS Secrets Manager to securely manage sensitive information, such as passwords, API keys, and certificates.

Example: Parameterization

Parameterize configurations in IaC templates to separate sensitive data from the code. This allows secure management of secrets outside the template.

Infrastructure Monitoring and Maintenance

Monitoring and maintaining infrastructure deployed through IaC require a proactive approach.

Example: Monitoring Integration

Integrate infrastructure monitoring tools, such as Prometheus or CloudWatch, to monitor the health and performance of IaC-managed resources.

Example: Regular Updates

IaC templates should be regularly updated to incorporate changes, improvements, and security patches. Regularly reviewing and updating templates is crucial for maintaining system reliability.

Documentation and Knowledge Sharing

Comprehensive documentation and knowledge sharing enhance collaboration and ensure that IaC implementations are well-understood.

Example: Template Documentation

Document IaC templates comprehensively, explaining the purpose, configuration options, and dependencies of each resource.

Example: Runbooks and Guides

Create runbooks and guides that detail how to deploy, manage, and troubleshoot infrastructure using IaC templates. This knowledge sharing ensures consistent operations and empowers teams to maintain the system effectively.

Continuous Improvement and Iteration

IaC implementations should align with the DevOps principle of continuous improvement.

Example: Post-Deployment Reviews

Conduct post-deployment reviews to evaluate the effectiveness and efficiency of IaC implementations. Identify areas for improvement, lessons learned, and opportunities to enhance the template's structure or configurations.

Example: Feedback Loop

Establish a feedback loop that encourages development and operations teams to provide input on IaC templates. Encourage suggestions for optimization, increased efficiency, and alignment with changing requirements.

Training and Skill Development

Effective implementation of IaC requires teams to possess the necessary skills and knowledge.

Example: Training Programs

Offer training programs that equip developers and operations engineers with proficiency in IaC tools, best practices, and template design.

Example: Skill Sharing

Encourage skill sharing within the team, enabling cross-functional collaboration and knowledge exchange. Developers and operations engineers can learn from each other's expertise.

Challenges and Mitigation Strategies

While implementing IaC offers significant benefits, challenges may arise that require strategic approaches.

Challenge: Learning Curve

Mitigation: Invest in training and workshops to help team members become proficient in IaC concepts and tools.

Challenge: Overcomplication

Mitigation: Start with simple templates and gradually incorporate complexity as your team gains experience. Keep templates modular and reusable.

Challenge: Legacy Systems

Mitigation: Integrate IaC gradually with legacy systems, creating IaC templates for new components or services.

Measuring Success and Impact

Tracking the impact of IaC implementation is essential to assessing its effectiveness.

Example: Deployment Time Reduction

Measure the time it takes to provision and configure infrastructure using IaC templates compared to traditional methods. A significant reduction indicates improved efficiency.

Example: Reliability Metrics

Monitor system uptime and incidents post-IaC implementation. A decrease in incidents and improved system stability signify the positive impact of IaC.

Conclusion: A DevOps Catalyst

Implementing Infrastructure as Code is a pivotal step towards realizing the DevOps vision. By selecting the right tools, establishing robust workflows, cultivating reusable templates, and incorporating security measures, organizations create an environment conducive to agility, reliability, collaboration, and continuous improvement. The benefits of IaC reverberate across the entire software delivery lifecycle, enhancing development velocity, reducing risk, and fostering a culture of excellence. As organizations traverse the DevOps journey, IaC stands as a catalyst that empowers teams to navigate the ever-evolving technological landscape with confidence, innovation, and a relentless pursuit of operational excellence.

Chapter 6: Monitoring, Logging, and Feedback Loops

Real-Time Monitoring and Performance Metrics: Navigating DevOps Success through Data Insight

In the fast-paced realm of DevOps, where agility and quality are paramount, the integration of real-time monitoring and performance metrics emerges as a cornerstone of success. The ability to gain insights into system behavior, identify bottlenecks, and ensure optimal performance in real-time empowers organizations to deliver with confidence and responsiveness. In this section, we will delve into the significance of real-time monitoring and performance metrics within the DevOps framework, exploring how they enable proactive issue resolution, enhance user experience, and drive continuous improvement.

The Value of Real-Time Insights

In the context of DevOps, real-time insights into system performance and behavior play a pivotal role in ensuring seamless operations and rapid response.

Example: Early Issue Detection

Real-time monitoring allows teams to identify anomalies, performance degradation, or errors as they happen. This enables swift issue detection and resolution before they escalate into critical problems.

Example: User Experience Optimization

Real-time insights provide a window into user behavior and experience. DevOps teams can promptly address performance issues that impact user satisfaction, ensuring a positive interaction with the application.

Proactive Problem Resolution

Real-time monitoring shifts the focus from reactive to proactive problem resolution.

Example: Predictive Analytics

By analyzing historical performance data in real-time, predictive analytics can identify patterns that indicate potential future issues. This proactive approach enables preemptive actions to prevent system outages.

Example: Capacity Planning

Real-time monitoring aids in capacity planning by tracking resource utilization trends. DevOps teams can anticipate resource shortages and scale up infrastructure before performance is compromised.

Visibility into Microservices

In a microservices architecture, real-time monitoring becomes even more critical.

Example: Service Dependencies

Real-time monitoring allows teams to visualize service dependencies and interactions. When a service experiences issues, it's easier to identify the root cause and mitigate impact on other services.

Example: Rapid Debugging

In a microservices environment, issues can be distributed across services. Real-time monitoring enables rapid debugging by pinpointing the specific service causing the problem.

Continuous Improvement and Iteration

Real-time monitoring facilitates a continuous improvement cycle by providing data-driven insights.

Example: A/B Testing

Real-time monitoring allows teams to conduct A/B testing in production environments. By comparing the performance and user engagement of different versions, teams can make informed decisions to optimize applications.

Example: Feedback Loop

Performance metrics obtained in real-time contribute to the feedback loop. Teams can analyze metrics to understand the impact of code changes, identify performance regressions, and make adjustments.

Choosing Relevant Performance Metrics

The selection of performance metrics is crucial in obtaining actionable insights.

Example: Response Time

Monitoring response time provides visibility into how quickly the system responds to user requests.

Example: Error Rates

Real-time monitoring of error rates helps teams identify abnormal spikes in errors, allowing them to take immediate action to resolve issues.

Example: Resource Utilization

Tracking CPU, memory, and network utilization provides insights into resource bottlenecks. DevOps teams can optimize resource allocation for optimal performance.

Real-Time Monitoring Tools

Choosing the right real-time monitoring tools is essential for effective implementation.

Example: Prometheus

It offers a powerful querying language and visualization capabilities.

Example: Grafana

Grafana is a visualization platform that integrates with monitoring tools like Prometheus. It allows teams to create customizable dashboards to visualize real-time metrics.

Automated Alerts and Incident Response

Real-time monitoring tools often include automated alerting features.

Example: Alert Thresholds

DevOps teams can set thresholds for performance metrics. If a metric exceeds the threshold, an alert is triggered, enabling rapid incident response.

Example: Escalation Procedures

Automated alerts can be routed to the appropriate team members based on severity. This ensures that the right people are notified promptly.

Integrating Monitoring into CI/CD Pipelines

Real-time monitoring should be integrated into the CI/CD pipeline for continuous feedback.

Example: Performance Testing

Performance tests integrated into the pipeline can provide real-time data on how code changes impact performance. This helps catch performance regressions early.

Example: Deployment Validation

Real-time monitoring during deployment can validate the impact of changes on performance. If metrics deviate from the baseline, the deployment can be rolled back.

Conclusion: Navigating DevOps Excellence

In the dynamic realm of DevOps, where agility and quality are paramount, real-time monitoring and performance metrics stand as guiding beacons. The ability to gain insights into system behavior, predict issues, and optimize performance in real-time empowers organizations to respond swiftly, minimize downtime, and enhance user experience. By choosing relevant metrics, adopting appropriate monitoring tools, and integrating monitoring into the CI/CD pipeline, organizations pave the way for proactive problem resolution, continuous improvement, and operational excellence. As DevOps practitioners navigate the intricate landscape of software delivery, real-time monitoring and performance metrics become indispensable tools that drive them towards success with data-driven precision and strategic insight.

Logging Strategies for Troubleshooting and Optimization: Illuminating the Path to DevOps Excellence

In the intricate landscape of DevOps, where agility and quality are paramount, effective logging strategies emerge as crucial components of success. Logging provides a window into system behavior, enabling DevOps teams to diagnose issues, troubleshoot anomalies, and optimize performance. In this section, we will explore the significance of logging within the DevOps framework, delve into strategies for generating meaningful logs, and highlight how logs drive efficient troubleshooting, informed decision-making, and continuous optimization.

The Value of Logging in DevOps

Logging is more than a passive record-keeping process; it's a dynamic tool that empowers DevOps teams to gain insights, identify trends, and maintain system health.

Example: Issue Identification

Logs provide a trail of events, helping teams trace the sequence of actions leading to an issue. Analyzing logs can unveil root causes and facilitate timely issue resolution.

Example: Anomaly Detection

Logging enables teams to detect abnormal patterns, such as unexpected traffic spikes or increased error rates. These anomalies can signal impending issues that require immediate attention.

Generating Meaningful Logs

Effective logging requires a strategy that produces logs with relevant information.

Example: Contextual Information

Logs should include contextual information such as timestamps, user IDs, transaction details, and relevant metadata. This information enriches logs and aids in understanding the context of events.

Example: Log Levels

Implementing different log levels (e.g., DEBUG, INFO, WARN, ERROR) allows teams to control the verbosity of logs. This ensures that only relevant information is captured based on the severity of the event.

Structured Logging

Structured logging enhances the interpretability of logs by using a consistent format.

Example: JSON Format

Structuring logs in JSON format allows for easy parsing, filtering, and analysis. Each log entry becomes a structured object with well-defined fields.

Example: Key-Value Pairs

Logs can include key-value pairs that provide additional context to each log entry. This aids in quickly identifying relevant information within logs.

Log Aggregation and Centralization

Aggregating logs in a central location streamlines troubleshooting and analysis.

Example: Log Collectors

Log collectors such as Fluentd or Logstash gather logs from various sources and forward them to a centralized storage or visualization platform.

Example: ELK Stack

The ELK Stack (Elasticsearch, Logstash, Kibana) is a popular solution for log aggregation. Elasticsearch indexes logs, Logstash collects and processes logs, and Kibana provides visualization and search capabilities.

Contextual Correlation

Logs become more insightful when correlated with relevant events.

Example: Trace IDs

Assigning a unique trace ID to a transaction or request allows logs related to that transaction to be easily correlated, providing end-to-end visibility.

Example: Distributed Tracing

Distributed tracing tools like Jaeger or Zipkin enable tracing requests across microservices, offering insights into the journey of a request and the services it interacts with.

Alerting and Monitoring

Logs play a crucial role in alerting and monitoring systems.

Example: Log-Based Alerts

Set up alerts based on specific log patterns or error messages. When a predefined condition is met, an alert is triggered, prompting immediate action.

Example: Log-Based Metrics

Convert log data into metrics to monitor trends over time. For example, track the frequency of specific error messages to identify recurring issues.

DevOps Collaboration

Logs serve as a common language for collaboration between development and operations teams.

Example: Shared Understanding

Both teams can analyze logs to gain a shared understanding of system behavior, identify performance bottlenecks, and address issues collaboratively.

Example: Post-Incident Analysis

After an incident, logs provide a comprehensive record of events, enabling teams to conduct post-incident analysis, identify root causes, and implement preventive measures.

Continuous Improvement and Optimization

Logs are valuable tools for continuous improvement.

Example: Performance Tuning

Analyzing logs can reveal performance bottlenecks, allowing teams to fine-tune configurations and optimize resource usage.

Example: Capacity Planning

Logs provide insights into resource utilization trends, aiding in capacity planning and ensuring resources are allocated optimally.

Data Privacy and Security

While logs are invaluable for troubleshooting, privacy and security must be upheld.

Example: Log Redaction

Sensitive information such as passwords or personal data should be redacted from logs to prevent exposure.

Example: Access Controls

Implement access controls to ensure that only authorized individuals have access to logs containing sensitive information.

Conclusion: Enlightening DevOps Excellence

Logging strategies stand as beacons illuminating the path towards DevOps excellence. By generating meaningful logs, structuring them effectively, aggregating them centrally, and harnessing their insights for collaboration, troubleshooting, and optimization, organizations fortify their ability to deliver with precision and agility. In an era where technology's complexity requires a keen understanding of system behavior, logs serve as the guiding light that empowers DevOps teams to navigate the challenges and seize the opportunities of the ever-evolving digital landscape.

Incorporating Feedback Loops for Continuous Improvement: Iterating Towards DevOps Excellence

In the dynamic world of DevOps, the integration of feedback loops emerges as a vital strategy for achieving and sustaining operational excellence. Feedback loops facilitate the iterative process of learning, adapting, and optimizing, empowering DevOps teams to respond swiftly to challenges, make informed decisions, and drive continuous improvement. In this section, we will explore the significance of feedback loops within the DevOps framework, examine different types of feedback loops, and highlight how they foster a culture of collaboration, innovation, and relentless enhancement.

The Power of Feedback Loops in DevOps

Feedback loops provide a mechanism for DevOps teams to gather insights from various sources and apply those insights to enhance processes, products, and overall performance.

Example: Rapid Issue Resolution

Feedback loops enable real-time identification of issues. When users report problems, teams can swiftly analyze the feedback, pinpoint root causes, and deploy fixes.

Example: Data-Informed Decisions

Feedback loops provide data-driven insights that guide decision-making. By analyzing user feedback and system metrics, teams can make informed choices to optimize applications.

Types of Feedback Loops

DevOps embraces various feedback loops that span the entire software development lifecycle.

Example: Continuous Integration Feedback

In the CI phase, automated tests provide feedback on code quality and test coverage. This loop ensures that code changes adhere to quality standards.

Example: Continuous Deployment Feedback

Automated deployment pipelines provide feedback on the success of deployments. If a deployment fails, the loop prompts immediate corrective action.

Example: User Experience Feedback

User feedback and analytics offer insights into user satisfaction, behavior, and pain points. This feedback loop drives user-centric enhancements.

Example: Post-Incident Analysis

After incidents, post-incident analysis generates feedback on the effectiveness of incident response. Teams identify areas for improvement to prevent similar incidents.

Continuous Improvement through Iteration

Feedback loops are the catalysts for continuous improvement.

Example: Sprint Retrospectives

In Agile methodologies, sprint retrospectives gather feedback from team members. Insights are used to refine processes, enhance collaboration, and optimize productivity.

Example: Release Feedback

Feedback after a release informs future releases. Teams analyze user feedback, performance metrics, and incidents to refine the deployment process.

User-Centric Product Enhancement

Feedback loops enable organizations to create products that meet user needs.

Example: User Surveys

User surveys gather feedback on usability, functionality, and overall satisfaction. This input guides product enhancements that align with user expectations.

Example: Beta Testing

Beta testing provides an avenue for users to experience new features and provide feedback before wide release. This loop ensures that products align with user preferences.

DevOps Collaboration and Learning

Feedback loops foster a culture of collaboration and learning.

Example: Cross-Functional Collaboration

Feedback loops encourage communication between development and operations teams. Collaborative problem-solving leads to efficient issue resolution.

Example: Shared Learning

Incident post-mortems generate feedback on incident response. Sharing these insights across teams ensures that everyone benefits from lessons learned.

Automation and Continuous Integration

Automation is integral to effective feedback loops.

Example: Automated Testing

Automated testing generates rapid feedback on code changes. This loop ensures that defects are caught early, reducing the cost of fixing them.

Example: Continuous Integration and Deployment

Automated CI/CD pipelines provide real-time feedback on code quality and deployment success. Automated tests validate changes before they reach production.

Metrics-Driven Insights

Feedback loops are fueled by metrics that guide improvement efforts.

Example: Performance Metrics

Monitoring performance metrics provides feedback on system health and resource utilization. This loop informs scaling decisions and optimization efforts.

Example: Error Rates

Monitoring error rates generates feedback on application stability. Anomalies trigger alerts, prompting teams to investigate and resolve issues.

Creating a Feedback-Driven Culture

A feedback-driven culture is essential for DevOps success.

Example: Encouraging Feedback

Foster an environment where team members are encouraged to provide feedback on processes, tools, and collaboration.

Example: Celebrating Improvement

Acknowledge and celebrate improvements resulting from feedback loops. This reinforces the value of iterative enhancement.

Conclusion: Iterating Towards Excellence

In the DevOps journey, feedback loops stand as the compass that guides teams towards operational excellence. By incorporating various types of feedback loops, automating processes, leveraging metrics, and fostering a culture of collaboration and learning, organizations pave the way for iterative improvement. Feedback loops empower DevOps teams to navigate challenges, seize opportunities, and evolve with agility in an ever-changing technological landscape. As the heartbeat of continuous improvement, feedback loops are the driving force behind DevOps' commitment to relentless enhancement and a quest for excellence.

Chapter 7: Security and Compliance in DevOps

Integrating Security Throughout the Software Lifecycle: Fortifying DevOps with a Shield of Protection

In the era of DevOps, where speed and innovation are paramount, the integration of security throughout the software lifecycle emerges as a foundational imperative. In this section, we will explore the significance of integrating security within DevOps, delve into the key practices of DevSecOps, and highlight how this approach fortifies applications, safeguards data, and bolsters organizational resilience.

The Crucial Role of Security in DevOps

Security is no longer a standalone concern; it's an intrinsic element of DevOps that safeguards applications, data, and users.

Example: Vulnerability Prevention

By identifying vulnerabilities early in the development process, DevSecOps prevents security flaws from infiltrating production environments.

Example: Rapid Incident Response

With security integrated into every phase, teams can detect and respond to security incidents swiftly, minimizing damage and downtime.

Key Practices of DevSecOps

DevSecOps encompasses a range of practices that collectively create a security-first culture.

Example: Security as Code

Treating security configurations as code ensures that security measures are defined, versioned, and automated, just like application code.

Example: Continuous Security Testing

Integrating security testing into the CI/CD pipeline enables automated security assessments at every code change.

Example: Threat Modeling

Threat modeling assesses potential threats and vulnerabilities early in the development process, guiding security efforts effectively.

Shift-Left Security

DevSecOps embodies the "shift-left" approach, addressing security early in the development cycle.

Example: Static Application Security Testing (SAST)

Conducting SAST during code development identifies security vulnerabilities before code is merged, reducing the cost of remediation.

Example: Dynamic Application Security Testing (DAST)

Performing DAST during the testing phase identifies vulnerabilities in running applications, ensuring that security issues are resolved before deployment.

Continuous Compliance

DevSecOps ensures that applications adhere to security standards and compliance requirements.

Example: Automated Compliance Checks

Automated checks in the CI/CD pipeline validate that applications meet security and compliance standards before deployment.

Example: Infrastructure Compliance

Security configurations for infrastructure components are defined as code and undergo automated testing to ensure adherence to security policies.

Threat Detection and Response

Real-time threat detection and response are integral to DevSecOps.

Example: Intrusion Detection Systems (IDS)

Incorporating IDS tools into the pipeline detects anomalous behaviors that might indicate security breaches.

Example: Automated Incident Response

Automated incident response triggers immediate actions in response to security incidents, minimizing potential damage.

Container Security

Containerized applications require specialized security measures.

Example: Image Scanning

Automated scanning of container images identifies vulnerabilities and ensures that only secure images are deployed.

Example: Runtime Security

Runtime monitoring of containers detects abnormal behavior, unauthorized access, or potential threats during application execution.

Collaborative Security Culture

DevSecOps fosters a culture where security is everyone's responsibility.

Example: Security Training

All team members receive security training to understand potential risks and best practices.

Example: Security Champions

Appointing security champions within development teams promotes awareness and knowledge sharing about security practices.

A Shield of Protection

In the modern landscape of DevOps, integrating security throughout the software lifecycle isn't an option; it's a necessity. DevSecOps ensures that security is embedded into every facet of development and operations, from code creation to deployment and beyond. By implementing key practices, embracing the shift-left approach, focusing on compliance, and fostering a collaborative security culture, organizations erect a shield of protection around their applications and data. DevSecOps stands as a testament to the commitment to not only deliver with speed but also with unwavering security, resilience, and a dedication to safeguarding the digital landscape.

DevSecOps: Bridging Security and DevOps Practices for Unified Excellence

In the dynamic landscape of software development, where agility and security are paramount, the emergence of DevSecOps stands as a bridge that unites the domains of security and DevOps practices. DevSecOps represents a paradigm shift that not only accelerates software delivery but also integrates security into every phase of the development and operations lifecycle. In this section, we will explore the fundamental principles of DevSecOps, delve into its core practices, and highlight how this holistic approach fosters a culture of collaboration, risk mitigation, and continuous improvement.

The Essence of DevSecOps

DevSecOps is more than a mere amalgamation of development, security, and operations; it's a cultural and operational mindset that harmonizes these elements into a cohesive whole.

Example: Security as Enabler

DevSecOps views security not as a barrier but as an enabler of innovation. Security practices enhance agility rather than impede it.

Example: Holistic Lifecycle Integration

DevSecOps unifies security practices with the entire software lifecycle, ensuring that security is a continuous consideration from ideation to deployment.

Key Principles of DevSecOps

DevSecOps adheres to key principles that shape its implementation.

Example: Shift-Left Security

By addressing security early in the development process, DevSecOps minimizes vulnerabilities and reduces the cost of fixing issues.

Example: Automation

Automation is at the heart of DevSecOps. Automated security checks, tests, and compliance assessments ensure rapid and consistent security practices.

Example: Continuous Learning

DevSecOps embraces a culture of learning and adaptation. Incident post-mortems and feedback loops drive continuous improvement in security practices.

Embracing a Security-First Mindset

DevSecOps infuses security considerations into every aspect of development and operations.

Example: Secure Coding Practices

Development teams follow secure coding practices, adhering to guidelines that mitigate common vulnerabilities and ensure code quality.

Example: Continuous Security Testing

Security testing is automated and integrated into the CI/CD pipeline, guaranteeing that security assessments are an inherent part of the release process.

Example: Infrastructure as Code Security

Security configurations for infrastructure components are treated as code and undergo rigorous testing, preventing security gaps.

Collaboration and Communication

DevSecOps thrives on cross-functional collaboration.

Example: Security Champions

Security champions within development teams act as liaisons between security and development, ensuring that security concerns are effectively communicated and addressed.

Example: Shared Responsibility

A shared responsibility model ensures that security is not the exclusive domain of a single team. All members embrace security practices in their roles.

Continuous Monitoring and Adaptation

DevSecOps doesn't stop at deployment; it's a cycle of continuous monitoring and adaptation.

Example: Continuous Compliance

Automated compliance checks verify that applications adhere to security standards, and any deviations trigger immediate action.

Example: Anomaly Detection

Continuous monitoring tools detect anomalous behaviors, promptly alerting teams to potential threats or unauthorized activities.

Cultural Transformation

DevSecOps requires a cultural shift that values collaboration, accountability, and security.

Example: Security Awareness Training

All team members receive security training to understand threats, best practices, and their role in maintaining a secure environment.

Example: Continuous Learning

DevSecOps promotes a culture of continuous learning, where teams adapt and enhance security practices based on real-world experiences.

Conclusion: A Unified Path Forward

DevSecOps stands as a beacon that guides organizations towards a unified path of excellence, where security and agility coexist harmoniously. By embracing key principles, adopting secure practices, fostering collaboration, and prioritizing continuous learning, DevSecOps creates a synergy that fortifies software against threats while maintaining the rapid pace of innovation. In a world where digital landscapes evolve at unprecedented rates, DevSecOps ensures that security is not a compromise but an integral facet of every endeavor, cultivating a culture of resilience, adaptability, and a steadfast commitment to safeguarding the digital realm.

Ensuring Compliance and Auditing in DevOps: Navigating Regulatory Landscapes with Confidence

In the intricate realm of DevOps, where agility and innovation thrive, ensuring compliance and conducting rigorous audits stand as essential safeguards. DevOps doesn't merely prioritize speed; it also embraces the responsibility of adhering to regulatory requirements and industry standards. In this section, we will explore the significance of compliance and auditing in the DevOps landscape, delve into best practices for ensuring adherence, and highlight how this proactive approach not only mitigates risk but also fosters trust and transparency.

The Role of Compliance in DevOps

Compliance in DevOps goes beyond regulatory checkboxes; it reflects the commitment to ethics, security, and quality.

Example: Regulatory Adherence

DevOps teams must ensure that applications meet industry-specific regulations such as GDPR, HIPAA, or PCI DSS.

Example: Industry Standards

Adhering to industry standards like ISO 27001 or NIST ensures a robust framework for managing security, privacy, and risk.

Key Practices for Ensuring Compliance

DevOps teams employ practices that embed compliance into the fabric of software development and deployment.

Example: Infrastructure as Code (IaC)

Defining infrastructure configurations as code enables consistent and auditable deployments that adhere to compliance requirements.

Example: Automated Compliance Checks

Automated tools assess code and configurations for compliance violations, flagging issues before they enter production.

Example: Policy as Code

Writing compliance policies as code allows teams to validate adherence automatically, minimizing manual intervention.

Regulatory Audits in DevOps

Auditing in DevOps is a proactive measure that demonstrates a commitment to transparency and accountability.

Example: Continuous Monitoring

Continuous monitoring tools track changes, configurations, and access patterns, providing an audit trail for regulatory scrutiny.

Example: Automated Auditing

Automated audits provide detailed reports on compliance adherence, simplifying the process of demonstrating compliance to auditors.

Documentation and Traceability

Comprehensive documentation and traceability are crucial components of compliance.

Example: Versioned Documentation

Maintaining versioned documentation that outlines compliance controls, processes, and responsibilities ensures a clear audit trail.

Example: Change Logs

Detailed change logs record modifications to code, configurations, and infrastructure, facilitating accountability and transparency.

Cross-Functional Collaboration

Compliance is a shared responsibility that involves collaboration across teams.

Example: DevSecOps Collaboration

Close collaboration between development, security, and operations teams ensures that compliance concerns are addressed at every stage.

Example: Compliance Champions

Appointing compliance champions within teams fosters ownership and knowledge sharing regarding compliance requirements.

Auditing Strategies in DevOps

DevOps adopts strategies that streamline and enhance the auditing process.

Example: Immutable Infrastructure

Immutable infrastructure ensures that changes are versioned and auditable, allowing auditors to verify the state of systems at any point.

Example: Continuous Auditing

Continuous auditing, enabled by automated tools, provides real-time insights into compliance adherence, reducing the complexity of periodic audits.

Conclusion: A Path to Trust and Assurance

In the DevOps journey, compliance and auditing are not constraints but enablers of trust, security, and resilience. By embracing practices that ensure compliance, conducting proactive audits, and fostering cross-functional collaboration, DevOps teams lay a solid foundation of transparency and accountability. Compliance isn't a hurdle to innovation; it's a commitment to ethical practices and a testament to the dedication to delivering quality products while safeguarding sensitive data. In a world where regulatory landscapes evolve, DevOps' proactive approach to compliance becomes the cornerstone that instills trust among users, partners, and stakeholders, ensuring that the quest for operational excellence walks hand in hand with adherence to regulatory standards.

Chapter 8: Scaling DevOps for Large Organizations

Challenges of Scaling DevOps Practices: Navigating Complexities for Sustained Success

As organizations embrace the transformative power of DevOps, the journey towards scaling these practices can be both exhilarating and daunting. While DevOps offers the promise of enhanced collaboration, accelerated delivery, and improved quality, scaling these practices to meet the demands of larger projects, diverse teams, and complex infrastructures presents its own set of challenges. In this section, we will explore the key challenges that arise when scaling DevOps practices, delve into the complexities involved, and highlight strategies to overcome these obstacles and ensure sustained success.

Challenge: Cultural Transformation

Complexity: Scaling DevOps requires a shift in mindset and culture across departments and hierarchies. Teams that are used to siloed operations may resist this change.

Strategy: Leadership support, clear communication, and fostering a collaborative culture are essential. Encourage open dialogue about the benefits of DevOps and create shared goals that inspire collaboration.

Challenge: Tooling and Automation

Complexity: Scaling DevOps demands a robust toolchain that can manage diverse workflows, integration points, and environments. Compatibility issues and tool sprawl can hinder progress.

Strategy: Invest in a unified toolchain that supports automation, continuous integration, continuous deployment, and monitoring. Regularly assess and update tools to ensure they align with evolving needs.

Challenge: Managing Complexity

Complexity: As projects grow, complexity increases, leading to challenges in coordinating dependencies, deployments, and overall system behavior.

Strategy: Implement microservices and containerization to modularize applications, making them easier to manage and scale. Invest in orchestrators like Kubernetes to manage complex deployments.

Challenge: Compliance and Security

Complexity: Scaling DevOps introduces security and compliance challenges. Ensuring that security measures are consistently applied across a growing infrastructure can be complex.

Strategy: Implement security practices as code, integrate automated security checks in the CI/CD pipeline, and conduct regular security audits. Collaborate closely with security teams to align practices.

Challenge: Communication and Collaboration

Complexity: As teams grow and projects expand, maintaining effective communication and collaboration becomes challenging, leading to misunderstandings and delays.

Strategy: Foster cross-functional collaboration by creating clear channels for communication, promoting transparency, and conducting regular sync-ups. Use collaboration tools to streamline communication.

Challenge: Change Management

Complexity: Scaling DevOps can disrupt established processes and workflows, causing resistance and confusion among team members.

Strategy: Provide training and resources to help teams adapt to new ways of working. Communicate the benefits of DevOps and involve team members in the decision-making process.

Challenge: Monitoring and Incident Response

Complexity: As systems scale, monitoring becomes more complex, and incident response becomes challenging, potentially impacting user experience.

Strategy: Implement comprehensive monitoring solutions that cover all layers of the infrastructure. Automate incident response processes and conduct post-incident reviews to improve future responses.

Challenge: Scaling Team Skills

Complexity: Scaling DevOps requires scaling the skills of team members. As projects expand, teams must acquire expertise in new tools and practices.

Strategy: Invest in training and upskilling programs to ensure that team members stay current with evolving technologies. Encourage knowledge sharing and mentorship within teams.

Challenge: Consistency and Standardization

Complexity: Maintaining consistency and standardization across a growing number of projects and teams can become difficult.

Strategy: Define and document best practices, coding standards, and deployment processes. Implement automation and version control to ensure that changes are consistent and traceable.

Challenge: Monitoring Costs

Complexity: As the infrastructure scales, the cost of monitoring tools and resources can increase significantly.

Strategy: Optimize monitoring by focusing on essential metrics and automating routine tasks. Choose cost-effective monitoring solutions that align with your organization's needs.

Navigating the Path Ahead

Scaling DevOps practices is a journey that requires careful navigation of these challenges. By addressing cultural shifts, embracing automation, fostering collaboration, and maintaining a focus on security and quality, organizations can overcome the complexities of scaling and ensure that the benefits of DevOps are extended to larger projects and broader teams. While challenges are inevitable, they are also opportunities for growth and innovation. By remaining adaptable, learning from experiences, and continuously refining strategies, organizations can build a foundation for sustained success in the ever-evolving landscape of scaled DevOps practices.

Strategies for Enterprise DevOps Adoption: Guiding Your Journey with Hands-On Training

Adopting DevOps practices at an enterprise level can be a transformative journey, requiring careful planning and a comprehensive strategy. To ensure success, organizations should embrace hands-on training as a core element of their adoption strategy. Hands-on training not only empowers teams with practical skills but also fosters a deeper understanding of DevOps principles. In this section, we will explore strategies for enterprise DevOps adoption with a strong focus on hands-on training, providing a roadmap for organizations to navigate this journey effectively.

Strategy 1: Start with a Pilot Project

Hands-On Training Focus: Engage a small team in a pilot DevOps project. Provide hands-on training on tools, practices, and collaboration methods.

Benefits: A pilot project allows teams to experiment with DevOps practices in a controlled environment. Hands-on training ensures that team members understand how to apply concepts in real-world scenarios.

Strategy 2: Define Clear Objectives

Hands-On Training Focus: Conduct workshops to educate teams about the objectives and benefits of DevOps adoption.

Benefits: Hands-on workshops create a shared understanding of the goals of DevOps adoption. Teams learn how DevOps practices align with the organization's objectives and contribute to value delivery.

Strategy 3: Customize Training Paths

Hands-On Training Focus: Tailor hands-on training paths for different roles within the organization, such as developers, testers, and operations.

Benefits: Customized training ensures that each role gains the specific skills and knowledge needed to contribute effectively to DevOps practices.

Strategy 4: Collaborative Tools Exploration

Hands-On Training Focus: Provide hands-on sessions where teams explore collaboration tools such as version control, continuous integration, and automated deployment platforms.

Benefits: Hands-on exploration of tools fosters familiarity and confidence in using them for improved collaboration and efficiency.

Strategy 5: Continuous Learning

Hands-On Training Focus: Establish a culture of continuous learning with regular hands-on workshops, hackathons, and knowledge-sharing sessions.

Benefits: Ongoing hands-on training encourages continuous improvement and keeps teams updated with the latest DevOps practices and tools.

Strategy 6: Encourage Experimentation

Hands-On Training Focus: Encourage teams to experiment with new practices and tools in safe environments.

Benefits: Hands-on experimentation allows teams to learn by doing, understand the strengths of different approaches, and adapt practices to fit their unique needs.

Strategy 7: Monitor and Feedback

Hands-On Training Focus: Implement monitoring and feedback loops for training programs to gauge effectiveness and gather insights.

Benefits: Monitoring hands-on training effectiveness ensures that learning objectives are met. Feedback loops help refine training content based on the evolving needs of teams.

Strategy 8: Cross-Functional Collaboration

Hands-On Training Focus: Organize cross-functional hands-on workshops to foster collaboration between different departments.

Benefits: Cross-functional workshops build a cohesive understanding of DevOps across teams, enabling smoother collaboration and knowledge exchange.

Strategy 9: Share Success Stories

Hands-On Training Focus: Highlight success stories where hands-on training resulted in improved processes and outcomes.

Benefits: Sharing success stories demonstrates the tangible benefits of hands-on training and motivates teams to engage more actively in the adoption process.

Strategy 10: Continuous Improvement

Hands-On Training Focus: Incorporate feedback from hands-on training participants to continuously improve training content and delivery.

Benefits: Continuous improvement ensures that hands-on training remains relevant and valuable as DevOps practices evolve.

Empowering Enterprise Transformation

Hands-on training is not just a component of enterprise DevOps adoption; it's a catalyst for transformation. By adopting strategies that prioritize hands-on experience, organizations empower their teams with practical skills, foster collaboration, and cultivate a deep understanding of DevOps principles. As hands-on training becomes a cornerstone of the adoption strategy, organizations pave the way for a successful DevOps journey, marked by improved processes, enhanced collaboration, and a culture of continuous improvement.

Case Studies of Successful Enterprise DevOps Implementation: Learning from Real-World Experiences

Real-world success stories of enterprise DevOps implementation provide invaluable insights into the challenges faced, strategies adopted, and outcomes achieved. These case studies offer a practical glimpse into how organizations have harnessed the power of DevOps to transform their operations, improve collaboration, and deliver value at scale. In this section, we will delve into a few case studies of successful enterprise DevOps implementation, highlighting key takeaways that can guide organizations embarking on their own DevOps journey.

Case Study 1: Netflix

Challenge: Scaling infrastructure to meet global demand while maintaining reliability and innovation.

Strategy: Netflix adopted a culture of "Freedom and Responsibility," empowering teams to own their services and choose appropriate tools.

Outcome: DevOps practices enabled rapid deployment and experimentation, leading to features like chaos engineering for resilience testing.

Takeaways: Empower teams, embrace experimentation, and prioritize automation for rapid and reliable deployments.

Case Study 2: Amazon

Challenge: Accelerating software delivery while ensuring quality and security.

Strategy: Amazon embraced a "Two-Pizza Team" model, where teams are small enough to be fed with two pizzas, enabling agility.

Outcome: DevOps practices facilitated continuous deployment, enabling Amazon to release new features multiple times a day.

Takeaways: Foster small, autonomous teams, and build a culture of continuous deployment and iteration.

Case Study 3: Target

Challenge: Enhancing collaboration between development and operations teams to improve efficiency.

Strategy: Target focused on breaking down silos and fostering cross-functional collaboration.

Outcome: DevOps practices led to faster identification and resolution of issues, resulting in improved customer experience.

Takeaways: Prioritize collaboration, invest in shared goals, and align incentives to foster a culture of cooperation.

Case Study 4: Capital One

Challenge: Migrating to the cloud to increase scalability and flexibility.

Strategy: Capital One adopted "Cloud First" and DevOps principles for cloud migration.

Outcome: DevOps practices enabled Capital One to reduce time-to-market, enhance customer experiences, and achieve cost savings.

Takeaways: Embrace cloud technologies, and combine DevOps with cloud strategies for enhanced scalability and innovation.

Case Study 5: Google

Challenge: Managing complex, distributed systems while ensuring stability and innovation.

Strategy: Google embraced "Site Reliability Engineering" (SRE) to bridge the gap between development and operations.

Outcome: SRE principles ensured that Google services remained reliable, scalable, and efficient.

Takeaways: Implement SRE practices that emphasize reliability, automate operations, and encourage collaboration.

Case Study 6: Etsy

Challenge: Empowering developers to deploy and manage their code while maintaining reliability.

Strategy: Etsy introduced "Code as Craft," focusing on blameless post-mortems and continuous improvement.

Outcome: DevOps practices enabled frequent deployments while maintaining system stability.

Takeaways: Create a culture of continuous improvement, encourage transparency, and embrace post-mortems as learning opportunities.

Conclusion: Learning from Success

These case studies underscore the diverse paths organizations have taken to achieve successful enterprise DevOps implementation. While contexts vary, common themes emerge: empowering teams, fostering collaboration, embracing automation, and promoting a culture of learning. By studying these success stories, organizations can glean insights, avoid pitfalls, and tailor their DevOps strategies to suit their unique challenges and aspirations. The journey to enterprise DevOps excellence is marked by both challenges and triumphs, and these case studies illuminate the road ahead for those seeking to embark on their own transformative DevOps journey.

Chapter 9: DevOps Future Trends and Innovations

Emerging Technologies Shaping DevOps: Navigating the Frontier of Innovation

As the DevOps landscape continues to evolve, the integration of emerging technologies becomes a driving force behind its advancement. These technologies not only enhance existing DevOps practices but also introduce new dimensions of efficiency, speed, and scalability. In this section, we will explore the emerging technologies that are reshaping the DevOps landscape, providing organizations with tools and opportunities to elevate their software delivery processes to new heights.

Cloud-Native Technologies

Impact: Cloud-native technologies like Kubernetes and serverless computing enable scalable and flexible infrastructure.

Benefits: Automated deployment, scaling, and management of applications foster rapid and efficient development cycles.

Artificial Intelligence and Machine Learning

Impact: AI and ML facilitate predictive analytics, anomaly detection, and intelligent automation.

Benefits: Enhanced insights into application behavior, proactive issue resolution, and automated decision-making improve overall system performance.

Edge Computing

Impact: Edge computing brings computation and data storage closer to the data source, reducing latency and enhancing performance.

Benefits: Faster response times and improved user experiences for applications that rely on real-time data.

DevSecOps Tools

Impact: DevSecOps tools embed security practices into DevOps pipelines, shifting security left in the development process.

Benefits: Improved application security, reduced vulnerabilities, and compliance adherence from the earliest stages of development.

ChatOps and Collaboration Platforms

Impact: ChatOps integrates DevOps tooling with chat platforms, enabling seamless collaboration and incident management.

Benefits: Enhanced communication, faster incident response, and increased transparency among cross-functional teams.

Continuous Everything (CI/CD/CT)

Impact: Continuous Integration (CI), Continuous Delivery (CD), and Continuous Testing (CT) create a seamless pipeline for development and deployment.

Benefits: Streamlined development-to-production processes, accelerated release cycles, and improved quality assurance.

Infrastructure as Code (IaC) Evolution

Impact: IaC evolves with innovations like GitOps, allowing infrastructure configurations to be managed via version control systems.

Benefits: More granular control over infrastructure changes, improved traceability, and simplified management.

Serverless Architectures

Impact: Serverless architecture abstracts server management, enabling developers to focus solely on code.

Benefits: Reduced operational overhead, faster development cycles, and efficient resource utilization.

Immutable Infrastructure

Impact: Immutable infrastructure ensures that components are never modified after deployment.

Benefits: Improved reliability, easier rollbacks, and reduced configuration drift.

Quantum Computing

Impact: Quantum computing holds potential for solving complex problems at an unprecedented scale.

Benefits: Faster simulations, enhanced optimization, and breakthroughs in scientific and computational domains.

Embracing the Future

The DevOps landscape is in constant motion, driven by the infusion of emerging technologies that promise to revolutionize the way software is developed, deployed, and maintained. By embracing these technologies, organizations can harness new capabilities, elevate their DevOps practices, and stay ahead in the race for innovation. As emerging technologies continue to shape the DevOps frontier, organizations that proactively explore, experiment, and adapt stand to reap the rewards of increased efficiency, agility, and the ability to deliver value with unprecedented speed.

Predictive Analytics and AI in DevOps: Orchestrating Efficiency with Intelligent Insights

The infusion of Predictive Analytics and Artificial Intelligence (AI) into DevOps practices has ushered in a new era of intelligent automation and decision-making. By leveraging data-driven insights, DevOps teams can anticipate issues, optimize processes, and enhance overall operational efficiency. In this section, we will delve into the realm of Predictive Analytics and AI in DevOps, exploring how these technologies are reshaping the landscape and revolutionizing the way software is developed, deployed, and managed.

Predictive Analytics for Proactive Operations

Impact: Predictive Analytics uses historical data and patterns to forecast future outcomes.

Benefits: By identifying potential bottlenecks, performance issues, or failures in advance, teams can take preventive actions, reducing downtime and improving user experiences.

Example: Predictive Analytics can analyze application performance data and identify trends that could lead to performance degradation, enabling teams to allocate resources appropriately.

AI-Driven Automation

Impact: AI-powered automation enables the execution of routine tasks and decision-making without human intervention.

Benefits: Repetitive tasks such as environment provisioning, testing, and deployment can be automated, freeing up valuable time for more strategic activities.

Example: AI algorithms can automatically determine the optimal environment for testing based on historical data, accelerating the testing phase.

Anomaly Detection and Root Cause Analysis

Impact: AI can analyze vast amounts of data to detect anomalies and identify the root causes of issues.

Benefits: Swift identification of anomalies and accurate root cause analysis leads to faster incident resolution and minimized impact on users.

Example: AI algorithms can analyze logs, metrics, and events to detect patterns that indicate abnormal behavior, helping teams proactively address potential issues.

Continuous Improvement through AI Insights

Impact: AI-generated insights provide recommendations for process improvements and optimization.

Benefits: DevOps teams can fine-tune their processes based on AI-driven insights, leading to enhanced efficiency and quality.

Example: AI can analyze historical release data and suggest optimal release windows based on user activity patterns, minimizing the risk of disruption.

Enhanced Decision-Making with AI

Impact: AI assists in decision-making by processing complex data sets and providing actionable insights.

Benefits: Teams can make informed decisions related to architecture, scaling, and resource allocation, leading to optimal outcomes.

Example: AI algorithms can evaluate various deployment strategies and recommend the most suitable one based on resource availability and application requirements.

Conclusion: A Future of Intelligent DevOps

Predictive Analytics and AI have positioned DevOps on the brink of a transformative leap. By leveraging data-driven insights, organizations can elevate their DevOps practices to an intelligent realm where issues are foreseen, operations are optimized, and decisions are guided by factual analysis. As Predictive Analytics and AI continue to evolve, the DevOps landscape is set to witness even more sophisticated levels of automation, efficiency, and precision, ultimately paving the way for a future where the synergy between human expertise and intelligent insights yields unparalleled results.

The Evolution of DevOps Practices: Tracing the Path of Transformation

The journey of DevOps practices has been marked by a dynamic evolution that has revolutionized the software development and operations landscape. This subsection delves into the intriguing evolution of DevOps practices, highlighting key milestones, shifts in paradigms, and the overarching transformation that has redefined the way software is conceived, developed, deployed, and maintained.

Origins: Bridging the Divide

Early Phase: DevOps emerged as a response to the silos between development and operations teams.

Focus: The primary goal was to improve collaboration and communication, breaking down the barriers that hindered efficient software delivery.

Result: Increased cooperation led to faster releases, reduced errors, and better alignment with business goals.

Automation: Catalyzing Efficiency

Shift: The focus shifted towards automating manual processes in development, testing, and deployment.

Automation Types: Continuous Integration (CI) and Continuous Delivery (CD) became pivotal, automating build and release pipelines.

Result: Automation accelerated delivery cycles, reduced human error, and laid the foundation for DevOps as a cultural and technical practice.

Continuous Feedback and Improvement

Phase: Continuous feedback loops were established to improve processes continuously.

Emphasis: Regular feedback, testing, and monitoring enabled quick identification of issues and iterative enhancements.

Result: Enhanced software quality, rapid issue resolution, and an iterative approach that embraced evolving user needs.

Infrastructure as Code (IaC) and Beyond

Shift: The concept of Infrastructure as Code (IaC) gained prominence, treating infrastructure like software.

Advantages: IaC enabled consistent and repeatable deployments, aligning infrastructure management with code practices.

Result: Improved infrastructure agility, reduced configuration drift, and streamlined deployment processes.

DevSecOps: Integrating Security

Integration: DevOps expanded to encompass security considerations, giving rise to DevSecOps.

Focus: Security practices were integrated throughout the development lifecycle, shifting security left.

Result: Enhanced application security, early detection of vulnerabilities, and a proactive approach to risk management.

Microservices and Containerization

Shift: Microservices architecture and containerization revolutionized application deployment.

Advantages: Microservices enabled modular development, and containers ensured consistent deployment across environments.

Result: Scalability, agility, and efficient resource utilization became integral to DevOps practices.

Cloud-Native DevOps

Current Phase: Cloud-native technologies and serverless computing amplify the scalability and flexibility of DevOps.

Emphasis: Native cloud services, microservices, and serverless architectures offer optimized environments for DevOps practices.

Result: Seamless scaling, reduced infrastructure management, and accelerated innovation in the cloud era.

Conclusion: A Continual Voyage

The evolution of DevOps practices has been a continual voyage of transformation. From its roots in breaking down silos to its current state in the cloud-native landscape, DevOps practices have shattered barriers, streamlined processes, and elevated the collaboration between development and operations teams. The journey continues as DevOps embraces emerging technologies, adaptive methodologies, and a persistent commitment to efficiency, quality, and user-centricity. As the digital landscape evolves, so too does DevOps, adapting and innovating to meet the ever-changing demands of modern software development and operations.

Chapter 10: Mastering Linux Utilities: Streamlining Operations for Efficiency and Productivity

Welcome to Chapter 10 of our exciting journey through the world of DevOps! In this chapter, we're diving deep into the realm of Linux utilities, where efficiency, productivity, and the joy of mastering the command line await you. Get ready to embark on a learning adventure that will empower you to navigate the Linux environment with confidence and finesse.

Unleashing the Power of Linux Utilities

Linux, the open-source operating system, is a cornerstone of DevOps practices. Its robust command-line interface provides a playground for professionals seeking efficiency and control. By mastering Linux utilities, you're not just learning commands; you're gaining the ability to wield the full potential of your system.

Benefits:

- **Efficiency:** Command-line tools empower you to accomplish tasks quickly, bypassing graphical interfaces.

- **Flexibility:** The command line offers unparalleled control over system operations and configurations.

- **Portability:** Linux utilities are accessible across various distributions, making your skills universally applicable.

Navigating the Command Line Landscape

Before we dive into specific utilities, let's get comfortable with the command line. Imagine it as your canvas, and commands as your artistic strokes. We'll explore basic commands, file navigation, and shell environments. You'll be surprised how quickly you'll adapt and feel at home in this dynamic space.

Experience:

- **Joy of Discovery:** Each command mastered opens up new possibilities, making learning a thrilling journey.

- **Command Fluency:** The more you practice, the more fluid your interactions with the command line become.

- **Error Tolerance:** Mistakes are part of the process.

Essential Linux Utilities

Get ready to meet your toolkit of Linux utilities that form the backbone of DevOps workflows. From text manipulation to file management, these tools are your trusty companions in your journey toward streamlined operations.

Key Tools:

- **grep:** Find and extract specific patterns within text, making data analysis a breeze.

- **sed:** Streamline text transformations, paving the way for automated edits in scripts.

- **awk:** Master data extraction, manipulation, and reporting like a pro.

- **rsync:** Efficiently synchronize and transfer files between directories and systems.

Supercharging Productivity with Pipelines and Redirections

Now that you're familiar with essential tools, let's supercharge your productivity by connecting them through pipelines and redirections. This dynamic duo enables you to create powerful sequences of commands, turning intricate tasks into elegant solutions.

Perks:

- **Efficiency Amplified:** Pipelines allow you to chain commands, creating complex workflows with ease.

- **Data Flow Mastery:** Redirect input and output streams to precisely control data flow between commands.

- **Problem-Solving Magic:** Tackle multifaceted challenges by combining tools into seamless pipelines.

Navigating the Filesystem like a Pro

Efficiently traversing and managing the filesystem is a hallmark of a Linux expert. Learn how to move, copy, and manipulate files and directories with grace.

Rewards:

- **Organizational Prowess:** Master file and directory operations to maintain a tidy and efficient workspace.

- **Scripting Potential:** Harness your skills in automated scripts, reducing manual intervention.

- **Rapid Adaptation:** Once you understand the logic, working with different directories becomes second nature.

Unlocking Administrative Powers

As you elevate your Linux utility skills, you'll naturally venture into administrative territory. Learn to manage users, permissions, and system configurations seamlessly.

Gains:

- **System Mastery:** Empower yourself to manage user accounts, groups, and permissions effectively.

- **System Customization:** Configure system settings to align with your specific needs and preferences.

- **Security Confidence:** Understanding user privileges enhances system security, mitigating risks.

Real-Life Applications and Projects

To truly cement your skills, we'll dive into real-life scenarios and projects. From automating tasks to data processing, you'll have the chance to apply your newfound expertise in practical, meaningful ways.

Highlights:

- **Real-World Impact:** Solving real problems reinforces your confidence and ignites your passion for Linux utilities.

- **Project Pride:** Completing projects boosts your sense of accomplishment and demonstrates your competence.

- **Learning with Purpose:** Apply your skills in contexts that matter, deepening your understanding of their practical implications.

Embrace the Joy of Mastery

As you journey through this chapter, remember that mastering Linux utilities is about more than just commands and syntax. It's about honing a skill that empowers you to streamline operations, optimize workflows, and tackle challenges with elegance. So, immerse yourself in the world of Linux, relish the joy of discovery, and embrace the excitement of becoming a Linux command-line maestro!

Key Takeaways:

- Linux utilities empower you with efficiency, flexibility, and portability.

- Navigating the command line is an exciting journey of adaptation and fluency.

- Essential Linux utilities like grep, sed, awk, and rsync are your go-to tools.

- Pipelines and redirections supercharge your productivity.

- Mastery of filesystem navigation and administrative tasks elevates your skillset.

- Real-life applications and projects solidify your expertise and confidence.

Get ready to experience the exhilaration of mastering Linux utilities—your ticket to enhanced efficiency and productivity in the dynamic world of DevOps!

Linux Utilities: Unleashing Efficiency, Flexibility, and Portability

In the realm of DevOps, Linux utilities stand as the unsung heroes that empower professionals to achieve feats of efficiency, flexibility, and portability. These tools, embedded within the command-line interface, hold the key to unlocking a world of streamlined operations and seamless interactions with your system. Let's explore how Linux utilities infuse your journey with their transformative qualities.

Efficiency: Accelerating Operations

Linux utilities are the accelerators that propel your workflow forward. When armed with the right commands, you can swiftly accomplish tasks that might otherwise require multiple steps through graphical interfaces. The command line's succinct nature fosters direct communication with your system, enabling you to achieve in seconds what might take minutes through alternative methods.

Benefit:

- **Rapid Execution:** Execute commands without the overhead of navigating graphical interfaces.

- **Precise Control:** Fine-tune operations and configurations with specific command parameters.

- **Shortcut to Mastery:** Learning command-line utilities enhances your overall efficiency in the long run.

Flexibility: Adapting to Varied Scenarios

One of the most captivating aspects of Linux utilities is their adaptability. These tools aren't confined to a single use case—they thrive in diverse scenarios. Whether you're managing files, analyzing data, or automating tasks, Linux utilities seamlessly shift to accommodate your needs. This flexibility ensures that your skills remain relevant across different projects and environments.

Benefit:

- **Universal Application:** Skills gained with Linux utilities are transferable across various Linux distributions and systems.

- **Dynamic Solutions:** Use the same utility for different purposes, tailoring it to each unique situation.

- **Innovation Catalyst:** Leverage Linux utilities to devise innovative solutions, customized to your challenges.

Portability: A Unified Skillset

In the interconnected world of DevOps, having a unified skillset that transcends system boundaries is invaluable. Linux utilities offer this portability, equipping you with tools that function consistently across different platforms. Whether you're working on your local machine or within cloud environments, the familiarity of Linux utilities remains a constant.

Benefit:

- **Cross-Platform Mastery:** Linux utilities work seamlessly on various operating systems, including different Linux distributions and Unix-like systems.

- **Seamless Transitions:** Switch between environments without relearning tools, saving time and effort.

- **Collaboration Catalyst:** Unified skills enable smoother collaboration with team members working on different systems.

Conclusion: Your DevOps Arsenal

Incorporating Linux utilities into your DevOps toolkit is like gaining access to a treasure trove of efficiency, flexibility, and portability. These tools empower you to execute tasks swiftly, adapt to diverse scenarios, and maintain a unified skillset across platforms. As you navigate the command line, you're not just learning commands; you're embracing a powerful resource that propels your DevOps journey forward, one streamlined operation at a time.

Embrace:

- **Efficiency:** Experience the thrill of rapid task execution and precision.

- **Flexibility:** Tailor Linux utilities to suit the unique demands of each project.

- **Portability:** Possess skills that seamlessly span different systems and environments.

With Linux utilities by your side, you're ready to embark on a voyage of enhanced productivity and agile operations in the ever-evolving landscape of DevOps.

Navigating the Command Line: An Exciting Journey of Adaptation and Fluency

Embarking on the path of navigating the command line is akin to embarking on an exhilarating adventure. This journey of learning and discovery is marked by the thrill of adaptation and the gradual mastery of fluency. Just as explorers once charted uncharted territories, you are charting the unexplored terrain of the command line interface, where every command is a step toward command-line proficiency.

Embrace the Learning Curve

As with any new terrain, the command line might seem unfamiliar at first. Yet, this learning curve is the foundation of your journey. Each command you encounter is like a signpost pointing toward a deeper understanding. Embrace the challenge, for it is the initial phase that ignites the spark of curiosity and propels you forward.

Experience:

- **Curiosity Awakening:** Unfamiliarity kindles the desire to learn and explore.

- **Growth Mindset:** Approach challenges with a positive mindset, viewing them as opportunities for growth.

- **Incremental Progress:** Celebrate each small success, as every command learned is a victory.

The Art of Adaptation

Navigating the command line is not just about memorizing commands—it's about adapting to new syntax, structures, and patterns. Each command you encounter is a puzzle piece that fits into the larger picture of command-line proficiency. With time and practice, the puzzle becomes clearer, and you find yourself adapting effortlessly.

Engagement:

- **Problem-Solving Joy:** Solving command-line puzzles becomes a satisfying mental exercise.

- **Adaptive Thinking:** As you adapt to new commands, you enhance your cognitive flexibility.

- **Command Versatility:** With adaptation comes the ability to modify and combine commands creatively.

Mastering Fluency

Fluency in the command line is not a destination but a journey. As you spend more time navigating the command line, you'll notice a shift from conscious effort to intuitive execution. Commands that once seemed complex will roll off your fingertips effortlessly, and you'll find yourself orchestrating sequences of commands with finesse.

Achievement:

- **Elegant Execution:** Execute commands with the grace of an experienced navigator.

- **Time Efficiency:** Command-line fluency translates to quicker task completion.

- **Confidence Boost:** Proficiency breeds confidence, enabling you to tackle more complex tasks.

Command-Line Rituals

Just as explorers have rituals to navigate unknown lands, your journey through the command line will have its own rituals. These may include daily interactions, frequent practice sessions, and the exploration of new commands. Embrace these rituals, for they are the compass guiding you through your learning expedition.

Practice:

- **Daily Exploration:** Regular interaction with the command line reinforces your skills.

- **Experimentation:** Try out new commands and concepts to expand your knowledge.

- **Community Engagement:** Participate in online forums to learn from and assist fellow command-line enthusiasts.

Command-Line Mastery Awaits

Navigating the command line is not just about acquiring skills—it's about embarking on a transformative journey. With curiosity as your compass and adaptation as your guide, you'll progress from a curious novice to a confident navigator. This voyage of adaptation and fluency is an exciting path that promises both immediate rewards and the long-term satisfaction of mastering a powerful skill.

Embrace:

- **Curiosity:** Fuel your journey with a thirst for learning and exploration.

- **Adaptation:** Embrace the challenge of adapting to new syntax and patterns.

- **Fluency:** Strive for command-line proficiency through consistent practice.

Your command-line journey is an adventure that promises both personal growth and the mastery of a valuable skill. As you navigate this uncharted territory, remember that every command you learn is a step toward realizing your potential as a skilled command-line navigator.

Essential Linux Utilities: Your Go-To Tools for Command-Line Mastery

Imagine a craftsman's toolkit—each tool meticulously chosen for its specific purpose and efficiency. Similarly, in the world of DevOps, essential Linux utilities serve as your trusted tools for command-line mastery. Among these, the quartet of **grep**, **sed**, **awk**, and **rsync** shines brightly, equipping you to conquer a wide array of tasks with finesse and precision.

grep: Unveiling Data Patterns

Meet **grep**, your search companion in the command-line realm. This utility excels at ferreting out specific patterns within files and streams of text. Whether you're debugging code, analyzing logs, or researching data, **grep** is your ticket to extracting meaningful information with ease.

Application:

- **Code Debugging:** Locate specific code snippets or occurrences within large projects.

- **Log Analysis:** Identify relevant entries in voluminous log files for troubleshooting.

- **Data Exploration:** Isolate data subsets that match specific criteria for analysis.

sed: Transforming Text

Next in line is **sed**, the text transformation wizard. With its magic wand of text substitution and manipulation, **sed** enables you to automate edits, perform find-and-replace operations, and reshape text data according to your needs.

Usage Scenarios:

- **Automated Edits:** Modify files programmatically, such as replacing text patterns across multiple files.

- **Text Formatting:** Transform text data into structured formats for processing.

- **Streamlined Scripting:** Use **sed** within scripts to manipulate data dynamically.

awk: Data Mastery, Simplified

When it comes to data extraction, transformation, and reporting, **awk** emerges as the maestro. This utility allows you to dissect and analyze data, define custom actions, and generate reports—all within the confines of your command line.

Versatility:

- **Data Parsing:** Extract specific fields or columns from structured data.

- **Customized Actions:** Define logic to process and manipulate data elements.

- **Statistical Summaries:** Generate reports and summaries from large datasets.

rsync: Effortless File Synchronization

As you traverse the DevOps landscape, **rsync** is your ally for seamless file synchronization and transfer. Whether you're managing files within your system or orchestrating transfers across different machines, **rsync** ensures your data is where it needs to be.

Practical Applications:

- **Backup Strategies:** Safeguard critical files by synchronizing them to backup locations.

- **Efficient Data Transfer:** Copy files with minimal data duplication, optimizing transfer times.

- **Remote Operations:** Use **rsync** to move files between local and remote systems securely.

The Harmonious Symphony of Linux Utilities

These four essential Linux utilities—**grep**, **sed**, **awk**, and **rsync**—form a harmonious symphony of efficiency and control. Each tool boasts its unique capabilities, contributing to your prowess in the command-line arena. From exploring data patterns to automating edits, from text transformation to seamless synchronization, these utilities are the building blocks of your command-line success.

Embrace the Power:

- **Efficiency Amplified:** Speed up tasks that would be time-consuming through other methods.

- **Empowered Automation:** Automate repetitive tasks with precision and consistency.

- **Problem-Solving Versatility:** Tackle a wide range of challenges with confidence.

As you harness the capabilities of these essential Linux utilities, you're unlocking a realm of potential. With each command mastered, you're adding another tool to your toolkit, equipping yourself to navigate the diverse terrain of DevOps with confidence, efficiency, and an impressive command over the command line.

Pipelines and Redirections: Supercharging Productivity for Command-Line Maestros

In the symphony of command-line operations, pipelines and redirections emerge as the virtuoso performance that propels your productivity to soaring heights. These dynamic duos enable you to seamlessly orchestrate commands, manipulate data, and redirect input and output streams with finesse. As you delve into the world of pipelines and redirections, you're embarking on a journey of command-line mastery where complex tasks are elegantly distilled into efficient sequences.

The Magic of Pipelines

Imagine you're building a chain of commands, where the output of one command seamlessly feeds into the next. This seamless flow is the magic of pipelines. With the | symbol as your wand, you're transforming the command line into a conduit of efficiency.

Advantages:

- **Task Sequencing:** Chain multiple commands to create intricate workflows.

- **Data Transformation:** Direct output data from one command as input to the next for on-the-fly processing.

- **Streamlined Operations:** Complex tasks are broken down into digestible steps.

Application:

- **Data Analysis:** Filter and process data iteratively, applying various transformations at each stage.

- **Log Parsing:** Extract specific information from logs and execute successive operations on the extracted data.

- **Text Manipulation:** Combine commands to perform complex text manipulations efficiently.

Redirecting Streams with Precision

When it comes to managing input and output, redirections offer a realm of control. The <, >, and >> symbols are your navigational tools to channel input and output streams exactly where you need them.

Capabilities:

- **Input Redirection (<):** Direct input from a file rather than keyboard input.

- **Output Redirection (>):** Redirect command output to a file instead of the standard display.

- **Appending Output (>>):** Append command output to a file without overwriting existing data.

Practical Use:

- **Creating Files:** Generate files containing command output for future reference.

- **Logging Output:** Capture command output for documentation or troubleshooting.

- **Data Input:** Feed large datasets as input to commands for streamlined processing.

Synergy in Action: Pipelines and Redirections

When pipelines and redirections join forces, the result is a dynamic synergy that streamlines complex tasks with elegance. You can create intricate pipelines that not only process data but also guide it to specific destinations, optimizing your workflow from start to finish.

Benefits:

- **Structured Workflows:** Seamlessly connect commands to form structured sequences.

- **Data Control:** Redirect and store intermediate and final results precisely where needed.

- **Task Automation:** Automate tasks involving multiple commands, saving time and effort.

Scenario:

- **Data Analysis Pipeline:** Extract data with **grep**, transform it using **sed**, analyze it through **awk**, and save the final result to a file—all in a single pipeline.

Elevating Your Command-Line Craft

As you embrace pipelines and redirections, you're ascending to the ranks of a command-line virtuoso. The ability to choreograph commands into orchestrated sequences empowers you to tackle intricate tasks with ease. Whether you're analyzing data, parsing logs, or performing intricate text manipulations, pipelines and redirections are your partners in productivity, turning complex operations into a symphony of efficiency.

Embrace the Symphony:

- **Creative Sequencing:** Construct innovative pipelines to achieve unique outcomes.

- **Precise Data Flow:** Direct input and output streams with precision, optimizing information flow.

- **Complex Task Simplification:** Break down multifaceted tasks into manageable steps.

With pipelines and redirections at your command, you're stepping onto the stage of command-line mastery, ready to compose and conduct intricate command symphonies that showcase your efficiency.

Mastery of Filesystem Navigation and Administrative Tasks: Elevating Your Skillset

In the intricate dance of DevOps, proficiency in filesystem navigation and administrative tasks is akin to mastering graceful choreography. Just as a dancer moves with precision and fluidity, a DevOps professional navigates the filesystem and wields administrative powers with finesse. Let's delve into the significance of this mastery and how it amplifies your skillset in the DevOps arena.

Filesystem Navigation: The Dance of Precision

Navigating the filesystem is more than traversing directories; it's an art of precision and organization. Your filesystem is your canvas, and with commands like **cd**, **ls**, **pwd**, and **mkdir**, you'll create a symphony of directory movements that facilitate efficient work.

Benefits:

- **Efficient Workflow:** Quickly access relevant files and directories, saving time and effort.

- **Tidy Organization:** Create and manage directories with a structured approach for streamlined file management.

- **Scripting Potential:** Automate directory navigation within scripts for hands-free execution.

Expertise:

- **Rapid Exploration:** Navigate to target directories in an instant.

- **Reliable Directory Creation:** Craft directories confidently without error.

Administrative Tasks: The Power Play

In the realm of DevOps, administrative tasks hold immense significance. With commands like **useradd**, **chmod**, **chown**, and **systemctl**, you become a conductor of system configurations and privileges. Administrative mastery ensures smooth operations and secures your systems.

Advantages:

- **User Management:** Create and manage user accounts and groups for secure access.

- **Permission Control:** Assign granular permissions to files and directories, ensuring data integrity.

- **Service Management:** Initiate, control, and monitor system services for optimized performance.

Impact:

- **Security Assurance:** Safeguard system resources and sensitive data with proper permissions.

- **Operational Excellence:** Efficiently manage system services for consistent operations.

Filesystem and Administration in Harmony

The interplay between filesystem navigation and administrative tasks is a harmonious duet that enhances your DevOps proficiency. Imagine smoothly traversing directories to locate configuration files and skillfully using administrative commands to tweak settings. This synergy streamlines tasks, promotes best practices, and reinforces your credibility as a DevOps practitioner.

Collaborative Benefits:

- **Efficient Troubleshooting:** Navigate to logs and configuration files swiftly, aiding in issue resolution.

- **Enhanced System Control:** Fine-tune system settings to optimize performance and security.

- **Comprehensive DevOps:** The union of filesystem and administration empowers you as a well-rounded DevOps professional.

Elevating Your DevOps Journey

As you master filesystem navigation and administrative tasks, you're equipping yourself with a skillset that propels your DevOps journey. Whether it's swiftly moving through directories, configuring system services, or managing user access, your mastery ensures that your operations are smooth, secure, and efficient. Just as a skilled dancer commands the stage, your proficiency in filesystem navigation and administration commands commands the DevOps landscape.

Embrace the Mastery:

- **Navigate Intuitively:** Seamlessly traverse the filesystem, locating resources effortlessly.

- **Administrate with Confidence:** Configure systems and manage permissions assertively.

- **Unified Skillset:** Meld filesystem navigation and administration for a comprehensive DevOps expertise.

As you ascend the ladder of proficiency in filesystem navigation and administrative tasks, remember that your expertise is not just about commands—it's about orchestrating a performance of seamless navigation, precise configurations, and the harmonious symphony of a well-versed DevOps professional.

Real-Life Applications and Projects: Forging Expertise and Confidence

In the journey of DevOps, theory and practice intertwine to shape true expertise. The bridge between the two is built by real-life applications and projects, which serve as the proving grounds for your skills. As you immerse yourself in hands-on experiences, you not only solidify your expertise but also cultivate unwavering confidence in your DevOps abilities.

Applying Theory to Reality

The concepts you grasp from textbooks and tutorials truly come to life when applied to real-world scenarios. Real-life applications transform abstract theories into tangible solutions, allowing you to witness the impact of your actions firsthand. Whether it's automating a deployment pipeline, optimizing code integration, or securing a system, each application bridges the gap between knowledge and practicality.

Advantages:

- **Contextual Understanding:** Apply theoretical knowledge to actual situations, deepening comprehension.

- **Problem-Solving:** Tackle real challenges, refining your ability to strategize and troubleshoot.

- **Skill Integration:** Synthesize various concepts into cohesive, functional solutions.

Project Immersion: A Confidence Boost

Projects are your proving grounds—a space where you orchestrate complex solutions, piece by piece. Engaging in projects instills a sense of accomplishment, affirming that you possess the skill to overcome multifaceted challenges. With each project completion, your confidence blooms, and your belief in your abilities strengthens.

Benefits:

- **Concrete Results:** Transform abstract ideas into practical achievements, boosting confidence.

- **Milestone Marking:** Project completions serve as milestones on your journey of growth.

- **Skill Demonstration:** Showcase your competence to potential employers, clients, or collaborators.

The Learning-Doing Feedback Loop

Real-life applications and projects create a feedback loop—a continuous process of learning, doing, and refining. As you face roadblocks and uncover innovative solutions, you're building a reservoir of experience that's impossible to gain from theory alone. This dynamic loop propels your learning forward, fostering adaptability and an agile mindset.

Cycle Progression:

- **Action:** Engage in projects, implementing concepts and theories in real settings.

- **Challenge:** Encounter challenges and uncertainties, promoting critical thinking.

- **Innovation:** Devise innovative solutions, expanding your skill repertoire.

- **Reflection:** Analyze outcomes, identify areas for improvement, and adjust strategies.

- **Growth:** Iterate through the cycle, accumulating experience and growth.

Realizing the Full DevOps Spectrum

Real-life applications and projects allow you to explore the full spectrum of DevOps practices. From orchestrating deployment pipelines to monitoring system performance, from collaborating cross-functionally to optimizing code integration, each project is a window into a specific facet of DevOps. This immersion not only broadens your expertise but also nurtures a holistic understanding of the DevOps landscape.

Holistic Proficiency:

- **Specialized Skills:** Tackle specific challenges, honing skills tailored to different DevOps aspects.

- **Integrated Knowledge:** Understand how various DevOps components interact within the broader ecosystem.

- **Adaptive Approach:** Develop the ability to adapt your expertise to diverse scenarios.

Crafting Your DevOps Story

Real-life applications and projects form the narrative of your DevOps journey. They showcase your growth, your adaptability, and your ability to transform theory into practice. As you look back on the projects you've tackled, you're not only witnessing your evolution but also constructing a compelling story of expertise that resonates within the DevOps community and beyond.

Capture the Story:

- **Document Progress:** Maintain a portfolio of projects that highlights your growth.

- **Skill Evolution:** Track how your skills have evolved through the completion of diverse projects.

- **Storytelling:** Share your journey with peers, employers, or collaborators, inspiring others.

With each project you undertake, you're sculpting a narrative that speaks of your expertise, your tenacity, and your commitment to DevOps excellence. Real-life applications and projects aren't just milestones; they're the cornerstone of your DevOps legacy—a testament to your ability to turn knowledge into impactful action.

Conclusion

Embrace the DevOps Revolution

As we conclude this transformative journey through the realms of DevOps, you've delved deep into a universe where technology, collaboration, and innovation converge. From the foundational principles to the advanced strategies, from mastering Linux utilities to orchestrating complex pipelines, you've navigated the multifaceted landscape of DevOps with curiosity, determination, and a hunger for growth.

In the world of DevOps, you're not just an observer—you're an active participant in a revolution that's reshaping how software is developed, deployed, and managed. Your newfound expertise isn't just a set of skills; it's a compass that guides you through the challenges and opportunities that lie ahead.

As you walk away from these pages, remember that DevOps is not a static destination—it's a dynamic journey of continuous improvement and adaptation. The DevOps revolution is fueled by your willingness to learn, your ability to collaborate, and your dedication to refining practices.

Embrace the Journey:

- **Lifelong Learning:** Commit to continuous learning and growth, staying updated with the ever-evolving DevOps landscape.

- **Agile Mindset:** Embrace change and challenges as opportunities to innovate and improve.

- **Community Engagement:** Collaborate with fellow DevOps enthusiasts to share insights, strategies, and inspiration.

Your journey doesn't end here—it evolves. As technology advances, as methodologies transform, and as the DevOps landscape continues to unfold, you stand as a DevOps advocate, a pioneer of streamlined operations, and a catalyst for positive change.

Now, armed with the knowledge, skills, and insights gained from this exploration, you're ready to embrace the DevOps revolution and contribute to a world where efficiency, collaboration, and innovation harmonize to create a brighter future.

Embrace the Revolution:

- **Innovate:** Propose new ideas and approaches to enhance existing DevOps practices.

- **Lead:** Champion the adoption of DevOps principles in your projects and organizations.

- **Impact:** Contribute to a world where software delivery is agile, efficient, and transformative.

Your dedication to mastering DevOps has the power to shape the way software is developed and delivered, and in turn, influence the industries, organizations, and technologies of tomorrow. May your DevOps adventure be marked by growth, fulfillment, and the realization of your boundless potential.

Embrace Your DevOps Legacy.

References

1. **"Kubernetes: Up and Running: Dive into the Future of Infrastructure"**

   Authors: Kelsey Hightower, Brendan Burns, Joe Beda

   Published: 2017

2. **"DevOps for Dummies"**

   Authors: Emily Freeman

   Published: 2020

3. **"Introduction to DevOps"**

   Website: Coursera

4. **"DevOps Culture and Mindset"**

   Website: Pluralsight

5. **"Official Kubernetes Documentation"**

   Website: Kubernetes

These references serve as a solid starting point for your journey into the world of DevOps. They offer valuable insights, best practices, and practical guidance that will help you navigate the complexities of DevOps and become a proficient practitioner in this transformative field.

www.ingramcontent.com/pod-product-compliance
Lightning Source LLC
Chambersburg PA
CBHW070835070326
40690CB00009B/1561